Praise for Natasha Munson's *Life Lessons for My Sisters*

"*Life Lessons* is not only for 'sisters' but anyone searching for the answer to what matters most."

—Dennis Kimbro, author of *What Makes the Great Great*

"Few books say it better or simpler than this one. *Life Lessons* uncomplicates success and puts the choices at your fingertips in a language everyone can understand. . . . A must-read for all those who are serious about success at home, at work, and in the community.

—George Fraser, author of *Success Runs in Our Race*

"Natasha Munson has gleaned wisdom that flows through the power of her pen. Her words will soothe your soul, uplift your spirit, encourage your heart, and leave you bubbling over with hope and inspiration!"

—Marina Woods, Good Girl Bookclub

LIFE LESSONS
FOR MY SISTERS

ALSO BY NATASHA MUNSON

Spiritual Lessons for My Sisters

LIFE LESSONS
FOR MY SISTERS

Natasha Munson

*How to Make Wise Choices
and Live a Life You Love!*

NEW YORK

Library of Congress Cataloging-in-Publication Data

Munson, Natasha.
    Life lessons for my sisters / Natasha Munson.— 1st ed.
       p. cm.
    ISBN 1-4013-0805-8
    1. African American women—Life skills guides. 2. African American women—Conduct of life. 3. Young women—United States—Life skills guides. 4. Young women—United States—Conduct of life. I. Title

    E185.86.M948 2005
    647'.0082—dc22

                                                    2004062801

ISBN-13: 978-1-4013-0805-6

Hyperion books are available for special promotions and premiums. For details contact Michael Rentas, Assistant Director, Inventory Operations, Hyperion, 77 West 66th Street, 11th floor, New York, New York 10023, or call 212-456-0133.

FIRST EDITION

10   9   8   7   6   5   4

FOR ALL MY SISTERS

———

Here is what I wish
that you hold true to yourself
it is not selfish to love yourself
more than any other
it is the pillar of self-esteem
focus on your goals and ambitions
understand though that destiny
must be confronted
when you feel you have strayed from the path
know that at this time you are gaining strength
often referred to as experience
accept it and your goals will stay sharp
demand respect or it will not be given
uphold your honest mind
letting only the truth be your guide
then you will never have to watch your back
or remember what you said
hate no one due to color
always judge by states of mind
color is just like looks
it can be deceiving

always question your surroundings
answer your whys
acceptance too soon can enslave your mind
understand that spirituality is the glue
that holds you together
belief in God can get you through a lot
that is where your faith should lie
trust no one more than yourself
depend on yourself first
love yourself first
respect yourself
encourage yourself
be happy with yourself
then share that love

ACKNOWLEDGMENTS

I AM GRATEFUL TO GOD for taking me on this wonderful journey and changing my life in such an amazing way.

I thank and appreciate everyone at iUniverse: Your quality of work and commitment to my books have been exceptional. I would like to thank my wonderful agent, David Dunton, for all his help in making my dreams come true. Thank you to Kelly Notaras and everyone at Hyperion for giving my dream wings.

I extend a big spiritual embrace and a warm thank-you to those who have helped shape my spirit and those who help me with my mission to empower the community one spirit at a time. Thank you to all the bookstores, women's groups, libraries, churches, book clubs, schools, companies, associations, and organizations that helped my book get into the hands of readers. I am humbled by and grateful for all my readers who reach out to me with words of encouragement, prayers, and inspiring words.

Thank you to my family for showing me that strength is a blessing, laughter is essential, and love heals all wounds. To all the family members that chose to hold me up with love and prayer rather than bring me down with words, you know who you are, and I love you dearly and thank you so very much.

I am sincerely grateful to God for giving me another chance to get it right and for allowing me to guide the lives of the kindest person I know, Kenya Munson, and the strongest girl in the world, Mecca Munson-Brown. I look forward to seeing you both become powerful women.

To all my friends that help me to laugh during the bad times, love with all my heart, and become better just by being in their presence, your friendship has been a saving grace.

CONTENTS

| *Contents*

SHAPE YOUR LIFE

USE YOUR RESOURCES

KEEP YOUR FREEDOM

BE YOURSELF

PREFACE

I DON'T KNOW THE FATHER of my children. I mean, I don't know who he is anymore. When we met I thought he was wonderful. You could feel the energy of love in the air between us. I thanked God for bringing him into my life. I later found out that he thanked God that night too.

We talked so much, every night, since the first date. We talked for hours! We were so in sync, so right for each other. We became a couple. He was loving and sweet and considerate. He would call just to say "Did I tell you I love you today?" I remember how happy it made me feel to think I'd found someone special. I knew his goals, dreams, fears, nightmares. I knew what type of father he would be. I knew the man he would become and the type of husband he would be.

Then, within a year and a half, our relationship gradually began to fade away. I saw that he wasn't the man I wanted. He wasn't the man I could love forever. There was something tearing him away from me.

I cried many nights when I realized he didn't love himself as much as I loved him. My heart felt like it would break as I waited by the window wondering where he was. It hurt my heart when I found out that the guy I had thanked God for had lost his soul and desire to crack cocaine. There was nothing I could do to bring him back. Not crying, loving, screaming, or fighting. Nothing.

My being pregnant just sent him further away and sent me within myself, wondering where I had gone wrong. He began to look like a person without a soul. His eyes looked like glass. I couldn't see the love in them anymore. The person I loved was no longer in that body. The window to his soul had closed, and kicked me out.

Now, though I see him when our kids go to their grandparents', I don't know him. I don't know who he is or what he stands for. All I see is the shell of a guy I thought had so much potential to be a great man.

My love blinded me, but my spirit saved me. My spirit pulled me through that torment so I could regain my life and stop trying to save him.

The greatest lesson I learned from him is that while love is beautiful, you must know if that love is genuine. You have to know if he truly loves you or just truly needs to be loved. I also learned that actions speak louder than words. We have to do what we say we are going to do. An intention is nothing if we don't follow up on it with action.

Getting through that relationship involved a lot of introspection. I looked at myself a lot. I wondered how I got myself into that situation and how I was going to get out of it. I went through the gamut of emotions. I blamed myself for not seeing him for who he really was. I thought I was stupid. I thought I would never find love again because I just didn't know how to choose men and because now I was a single parent.

Then at some point I remembered what my friend Kevin had said to me once. He said, "Tasha, don't ever let anyone kill your spirit. That's the most beautiful thing about you." I thought of him being open enough to tell me that and I cried. I cried because I had let my life become a rut. I allowed myself to focus on a dead-end relationship. I was killing myself. I knew I wasn't being Tasha anymore. I was being pitiful. So I changed.

I knew I had to rely on myself to get out of my rut. I knew my spirit was too strong and that there was too much more I could accomplish in life. So I began to slowly live my life. And it was that relationship that changed me into the spiritual person I am now. It allowed me to feel appreciation and love for those who gave me caring and love. It gave me humility and showed me my strength. That relationship, though painful, changed my life.

I know we all can't just change. I do know that, prior to that relationship, I had very high self-esteem and regard for myself. I loved myself more than anyone in this world and knew without a doubt that no one was better than me. So I simply had to remember what I knew. This is the foundation given to me by God.

But every day I see women hurting as they deal with relationships that are killing their spirit and I wish I could say something to stop it. I wish I could tell each and every one of them to live for themselves. Every one of them should know that she is the best in this world, that she is a gift from God.

We should know that all of us make mistakes. But that does not make us stupid—it just makes us human. We all face obstacles and challenges—we just need to know how to deal with them. We all need to know how to tap into life and live it to its fullest. We need to know that God is within us.

As I was coming back to my senses, I decided to share my experiences. I wanted to alleviate some of the pain that others go through and share my knowledge. I wanted to help others love themselves. I decided to write something for my daughters: a little manual of things I think they should know, a guide that would tell them what I had gone through and what others have gone through so they could learn some lessons. But I also wanted a way to talk to them about things that aren't so easy to say face-to-face.

Many of our young girls are misguided and uninformed—especially about sex and relationships. We have to speak to them. We have to prepare them. We cannot pretend forever that they are cute little girls. They will be women soon enough and the more knowledge we give them, the more prepared they will be. An informed woman is powerful. So my goal is to tell them the truth about life by sharing both the lessons I had to learn and the universal lessons all women should know.

INTRODUCTION

THIS BOOK IS MEANT TO BE a resource, your personal guide through life. I want to tell you what I know, honestly and openly, so that you can experience a more fulfilling life. I know that everyone in the world has an opinion for you. They tell you who you are and who you should be. I want to break it down and help you design your life, for yourself and your own personal happiness.

This book is definitely not the be-all and end-all. You are not going to receive everything you need to know about life in this one handy dandy book. But you will be equipped with some of the knowledge you need to make wise decisions and live life to the fullest.

I am going to deal with many topics. I'm still relatively young myself, so I haven't been through everything. But a lot of stuff does happen in your twenties, let me tell you! So I made sure this book contains some advice, quotes, and poems to inspire you, motivate you, and get you out there living life. Oh, and did I mention, also make wise decisions?

God only knows life should come with a study guide. Now this is yours, from me, with love, and the hope that it helps you to create a life that is more wonderful and fulfilling than you could have ever imagined.

CREATE YOUR LIFE

THE ONLY WAY TO LIVE

———

Time is of the essence
when you're reaching for that dream
every decision matters
like signs in the road
guiding you
on your journey
think clearly
notice every subtle clue
let your spirit be your guide
to a life filled with love
find what you love to do
and do it well

THIS IS YOUR LIFE AND YOU DETERMINE THE OUTCOME

———

All your life you have been someone's child, someone's granddaughter, someone's friend. But now it is time to separate yourself and find out who you are. Every teenager goes through a period of getting to know herself. Some twenty-year-olds are still doing it. And older! But this time really is meant for you to stretch your spirit and learn about your purpose in life.

Right now you are very good at comparing. You know you're nothing like so-and-so or you would never do this or that. And that's what I want you to tap into. Who are you? Think about some of the situations your friends or people in your family are in. Would you deal with the same situation? Why not? What about you makes you different from others? Would you stay with a guy who cheated on you? A guy who called you names? Would you stay with a guy who had no money? Why?

Make a list right now of the things you simply would not tolerate. This list describes your character. This is who you are and what you represent. You want this list to truly reflect you, so think of every possible situation you can. Think of the things you don't want to happen in your life. For example, if you know you don't want to be a single parent, write that down and write down the reason why not.

Next write down a realistic list of your dreams and wishes. A realistic dream and wish list includes things you definitely want to happen in your life and even things you wish would happen in your life. So, begin with your dreams. What is your dream? Describe your dream life. Then add the "realistic" side—the things you will have to do to make those dreams a reality.

Now look at your two lists. What you have done is describe the person you are and the person you will become. Nothing on the lists is impossible. You can make anything happen that you want to—and you will. All you have to do is turn each dream into realistic steps.

Every dream you have is a whisper from God. It's your destiny. All you have to do is begin the journey. All you have to do to achieve what you want in life is know that God believes in you. God gave you your dream. All you have to do is make it become reality.

Now, you may think, But it's an awfully big dream. Please! God created the universe. Even if your dream is to become the next astronaut, it is not impossible. Don't think limited. Use your mind to your advantage and don't let anyone discourage you. No matter what happens in your life, keep your realistic dream and wish list and work on it. You owe it to yourself to find inner happiness.

LESSON

This is your life and you determine the outcome. No one can live your life for you. The best thing you can do for yourself and for others is to live your life. When you are happy with your life and your life choices, you pass that happiness on just by being yourself. So each day remember you are special. Each day hold true to yourself. And, most importantly, each day work toward making your realistic dream and wish list a reality.

DON'T LISTEN TO THE OPINIONS OF OTHERS

At 21
a man becomes a man
and a woman becomes a woman
but time will tell
the mind is not always even
with the physical
how do things look
when age is not equated
with wisdom

Opinions, opinions, opinions. Everyone has one. Everyone thinks they know exactly what you should do with your life. In their defense, they can see your life more objectively than you can. They can see the mistakes you've made and can possibly even perceive the mistakes you are about to make. But opinions are not dependable. You know why? Because everyone has one. So everyone you listen to will give you a different perspective on your life. They say, "Well, if I were you, I would do this."

If you want even a shred of happiness in this life, listen to what they're saying but remember this: They are not you. This is your life. So any decision you have to make is going to have to come from you. You know what's best for you; you just need to know that the advice you give yourself is the only advice you need.

I firmly believe that God talks to us through our intuition. You know, that little voice that tells you what is right or wrong or whether you should do something or not. That is God utilizing your subconscious to guide you in your life. And all you have to do is listen.

It is essential to your life that you listen to that little voice and that you know when to tune out the opinions of others.

LESSON

The best opinion is your opinion. Do not be afraid to make decisions for yourself.

EDUCATION UNLOCKS
YOUR DESTINY

———

*The difference
between the height
of achievement
and the lows
of mediocrity
lies entirely
in decision*

I know when you hear this you tend to tune out. You think, Yeah, education is everything and a mind is a terrible thing to waste. I have no intention of wasting my mind, so I guess I'm a step ahead, and yadda, yadda, yadda. But education is much more important than you can ever imagine. Education unlocks your destiny. That means what you put into your education is what you will get out of life.

To determine your educational plan (college, trade school, or business venture), you first have to decide where you want to be in life. You have to think realistically about what you want to do. What impact do you want to make in this life? You cannot live life through others or for others. So the best decision you can make is to take your education seriously. Study as if your life depended on it. As much interest as you take in your looks and your clothes, take even more interest in your education.

What is education? Education is a learning experience that changes your outlook or thinking pattern. Education can make a fundamental difference in your life.

To help you make the best educational choices after high school, ask some friends and family members what they think your strengths and weaknesses are. You will be amazed at how well some people can point out things about you that you might not have noticed. Once you hear what they believe your strengths to be, think about their opinion. What do the strengths say about your character? What type of career can you see yourself in with these types of strengths? Remember not to limit yourself—there are more opportunities in the world than being a nurse or a lawyer. Open your mind to the many career possibilities out there. The goal is to find something you love to do, not something you have to do.

If you could be anything, what would you be? No, not rich! What would you do? Great, that's your goal, that's your dream. Now you have to make it a reality. It is your responsibility—not your mom's, not your dad's—to find out how to make your dream come true. So write down what your dream job would be. Then think of ways to make that dream a reality. Do you need to attend college? Do you need money to start? What do you realistically need? Do you need a mentor, someone who has been there, done that? Think of every possible way to make your dreams happen. Even if they feel unrealistic and far-fetched now, write them down. You are on your way to happiness.

Once you have a list of what you can do to make your

dream become reality, the next step is something many people never do. You have to begin. You have to pick something on that list and do it. Whether it's approaching a businesswoman and asking if she can mentor you or attending a workshop—make it happen!

LESSON

Take education seriously. It is the catalyst to changing your life and making your dreams reality. If you want a better life, you have to study and work toward it.

WELCOME TO MY LIFE

———

I say this is my life
and you stop telling me what to do
I say this is my life
and you stop telling me what to do
I say this is MY life
and you stop telling me what to do
No, I'm not whining
I'm trying to get through
this is my life
and I run this show
this is my life
and I know
what I want
I don't need you to tell me
I feel it in my heart
I'm on a mission
please don't stand in my way
this is my life
and I must run it
so that I may love it

BE THE CHOOSER,
NOT THE CHOSEN

If you let it, life will overtake you. Things will happen in your life and you will have no control. You will simply go from job to job, man to man, situation to situation, because you are allowing others to dictate your life. All your life people have been telling you what to do. Your parents, your grandparents, and your friends have all given you advice on what to do. And you listen because you know they mean well. But what you have to do now is listen to yourself.

Every person is put here to fulfill a spiritual purpose. We all have something to contribute to this life. But listen to your inner voice. You know—that voice that tells you what's right and wrong for you. Listen. Please listen.

That little voice is the best gift you have. That little voice is your intuition. Intuition is God. This is how he talks to you. You have a direct connection with the most powerful force in the universe. You can tap into that power at any time, for any question, and you will be guided to the right answer for you. There is nothing outside of you—not friends or family—that can answer your questions better than that little voice.

Your little voice is your spiritual guide. It will help you to make decisions and live life to the fullest. This is what you want. You want to live life to the fullest. The last thing you want to do is be unhappy, right? So let me tell you again, LISTEN.

Listening to your inner voice, your intuition, gives you the power of God. In essence you have the power to create your life. Remember what I said: You have the power to create your life. Every decision you make determines your future. From picking the right boyfriend to the best school, each decision is a turning point in your life.

Think of your decisions as milestones along the road. Your destination is happiness and success. So your decision-making is extremely important. Number one, you have to know where you're going. Where do you want to be? Number two, you have to think of the best route. Number three, when there's an obstacle, and there will be obstacles, you have to think of another way to get there.

Understand that life isn't meant to be difficult; it's meant to be a learning experience. The decisions and choices you make determine what you will learn. Your response to the obstacles that confront you will determine whether you settle and become complacent or whether you keep moving forward.

LESSON

Make every decision as if your life depended on it. One day you will see, your life, your happiness, your success, depend on the decisions and choices you make.

WHERE DO DREAMS GO?

———

What ever happened to that dream
that was deferred
was it bought off
like the people in this land
or did it sit and become glop
to be eaten by the never-minds
and won't-works
was that dream ever real
or in fact a true case
of figment of the imagination

GETTING CAUGHT UP IN
DAY-TO-DAY LIFE

———

Once you get out of the house and are on your own, it is very easy to get caught up in life. You get accustomed to paying the bills, maybe seeing a movie, hanging with the girls, or spending time with your man. This cycle of redundancy will continue for as long as you let it. Let me just tell you, it is easy to become stagnant.

You can have hopes, dreams, and goals, but if you allow yourself to get caught up in day-to-day dramas, all your ambitions will seem less attainable. You have to give yourself and the pursuit of your dreams top priority. That is not to say that your loved ones aren't important. This is just to state that, in your life, you are your top priority. And, believe me, there is nothing wrong with putting yourself first.

I'm not telling you to be selfish and be all about me, me, me. But definitely give yourself time to live. Realistically, you only get one shot at this life. The decisions you make each and every day will determine the outcome of your life. Do you really want your day-to-day struggle to be the pinnacle of your life? Believe me, no one ever said: "Wow, that girl never did anything with her life, but she sure could pay some bills!" The only person focusing on your bills is you, so you're going to have to shift that focus to getting out of your rut, living life, and making your dreams happen.

Remember, the only things that stay constant are the things that you allow to remain constant. Give yourself a break, all right? Live life.

LESSON

Whatever you focus on is what you will have and what you will get. If you want more out of life, focus your energy and time on achieving it. Visualize the life you want and make it happen. Let someone else focus on the day-to-day drama.

KNOW YOURSELF

SOUL MATE

His spirit is so strong
yet gentle enough
to share
to laugh
to hold
to be with

He is sweet
and considerate
in a way that is so loving
and so supportive
you feel like you've known him
all your life

He is reliable

Finally someone
who meets the definition of *man*
he's the one women dream about
and here he is

with a smile
that makes your heart melt

Eyes of wonder
and sensuality
and an embrace
that makes you feel like gold
but really
he's the gem

THE IDEAL MAN

According to books and television, women everywhere are looking for Mr. Right. They're fighting over him, sharing him, stealing him, doing everything they can to get him. And who is this "him"? Who is Mr. Right? Well, if he's your Mr. Right, you won't have to fight, lie, steal, or cheat to get him. He will be right there in your life at the right time. When or if he enters your life is totally up to you.

Before you go on your search for Mr. Right, you'd better make sure you're Ms. Right. Sometimes we hold ourselves up to some very high ideals. We see ourselves in a way that is not totally accurate. If you don't have your stuff together, the only person who will not know is you. Everyone else knows that you have issues.

The best thing you can do in this life is take some time for you. That does not mean five minutes in the bathroom. I mean take some time to get to know yourself. See what type of person you are without a man. Finding a Mr. Right with money might help you out financially, but it's not going to change whatever issues you were dealing with before you met him. Keep it real with yourself and don't expect anyone but you to fulfill your life.

When you take time for yourself and get to know you, you bring your best self into a relationship. Because then you know you can rely on yourself, you love yourself, and you are happy with yourself. Until you can do these three things, you aren't doing anything but wasting your time trying to find Mr. Right, because you're not Ms. Right yet.

Becoming Ms. Right does not mean attaining a state of perfection. No one is perfect. What it does mean, though, is that you love yourself, you are not holding on to any ill feelings, and you don't hate anyone. You are simply going for the best in life and are willing to open yourself to loving.

God gave you the world as a gift and you are a gift to this world. The ideal woman is someone who realizes that this world was created for her. She wants her life to have definition and for her spiritual purpose to be fulfilled. She is always willing to learn and to teach. She gives of herself lovingly, but carefully. She knows that no one in this world can fulfill her unless she loves herself first.

The ideal man will love you for who you are now. He will not find fault in you. He will not try to bring you down. He will be your friend, your lover, and your partner.

LESSON

The ideal man is someone who complements your life and wants to see you make yourself a better person. He is someone with whom you can love, learn, laugh, play, and grow. He is a man who will stimulate you to reach your highest goals.

I AM MY TRUTH

When I keep silent
am I helping you
or hurting myself

My God knows
I am killing myself
when I don't tell you
exactly where what
when and why

I'm limiting my mind
and allowing you
to define me
when I know what I believe

Holding in my words
is like holding in my breath
I will suffocate my spirit
if I don't tell you my truth

My truth is me
I am my truth
they cannot be separated
so I will speak

KNOW WHAT YOU STAND FOR

The saying "If you don't know what you stand for, you will fall for anything," is pure truth. In this life, you have to know what you want. You have to be able to look at yourself realistically. And, most importantly, you have to be able to look at others realistically. You have to understand the motivations and desires behind people's actions.

Many people go through life on autopilot. They have no desire to go beyond a certain place in life. They are comfortable. Therefore their entire lives are focused on the day-to-day. The focal point of their conversation is themselves or their relationships. Anything beyond that does not exist or is simply not important to them. Can you realize the magnitude of that?

Thinking only of yourself and the relationship you're in limits your spirit, your growth, and your life. This is your life. You have to know what you will and will not stand for. You have to want more than any other person you know. You have to want the best. Work for the best. Achieve the best. It is so important that as soon as you know what you want out of life you immediately begin working toward it. Never forget that it's a blessing to even know what you want and it's a reward to achieve it.

LESSON

In order to have a fulfilling life and make confident, wise choices, you have to know what you will and will not stand for in life. You have to be unwavering in your decision to be yourself and stand up for your truth. If you don't totally agree with someone, say so. Don't mislead or compromise yourself so that others may feel comfortable. Speak your truth. Live your truth.

OVERCOMING OBSTACLES

———

The challenges of life are ever-changing
when confronted with an obstacle
speak yell shout push pull kick hit
to move the obstacle
to do nothing
leaves you unchallenged
limited
and a fool

Anything you allow to block your path toward greatness is an obstacle. Any person or situation that gets in your way must be removed. This does not mean you use greed or malicious means to get what you want. Rather, take the desire for a better life that exists within you and make your dreams happen.

We are all always learning and always striving for more. You are just beginning. When people come to you with negative energy and negative thoughts, shake it off. Literally take a deep breath and blow it out. The more you allow the opinions and thoughts of others to affect you, the longer it will take for you to achieve your dream.

Look at the motivations of others. See if they are with you or not and then make the proper decision. It is essential to know when to let people go. Some people are not willing to work hard for their goals. Wish them well and send them on their way. Never let anyone get between you and your dream.

There's no one in this world more important than your happiness. Because once you've achieved a dream you will be a happier person and will be able to spread that to others. No matter what happens in life, do not let anyone deter you from achieving your dream. Your dream is your purpose in life. You have to fulfill it.

LESSON

There will be situations that seem insurmountable. There will be obstacles that you will feel are too difficult to get around. Everything you believe becomes the truth. If you believe an obstacle will remain an obstacle, it will. If you believe there is a way to get past an obstacle, you will find the way.

HEAVEN ON EARTH

Even with everything
something can be missing

Your heart may long for
fulfillment

Your soul may want
to love

Your breath may need
to coincide with a loved one

The deepest moment
that fulfills
bringing the happiness of heaven
is the love of
your soul mate

KNOW YOUR DEFINITION
OF HAPPINESS

———

We often hear, but don't always comprehend, the truth that happiness lies within. So I want you to hear yourself as you say out loud: "Happiness is within me, happiness is within me, happiness is within me."

Where's happiness? Exactly, it's within you. That means that in order to be happy and fulfilled, you have to fill your own needs. You have to follow your heart, pursue your dreams, and listen to yourself. We can make some of our most foolish mistakes based on the advice of others. You have to do what feels right for you. Don't let anyone mislead you or talk you out of your dreams. Happiness is your choice. Your decisions, your choice in friends, everything will decide your happiness.

Someone once told me, misery loves company. I was like, whatever. I knew his intentions were good when he tried to give me this advice. But I had no idea of what he was really saying until I was out of the situation I was in and could look back on it. I realize now that not everyone in this world wants to be happy. That's right. People will keep themselves in the same situations and keep making the same foolish choices. Your life can go around in circles as you do the same things over and over, or it can keep moving forward and getting better. It's all up to you. This is your life.

So for your happiness, decide who you will and will not be

around. Don't waste your time thinking you can change anyone in your life, especially a man. Don't love a man for his potential, love him for who he is. You will get your heart broken
and maybe your wallet busted if you love a man for what you
think he will one day become. There are some exceptions out
there, I guess. But don't rely on it. Love the man for who he is
now. If you can do that, then you are in love. If you're saying,
"Well, things would be better if he was just this or that,"—
uh-uh, get out of that situation, ASAP.

The way you spend your time and the people you spend
that time with directly affect your happiness. There are people
who bring nothing but negative energy to a situation: "We
can't do this and we can't do that." You need to drop them
quick-fast. Then there are those sister friends that you love, but
you're loving them for their potential too.

Sometimes we give our friends even more benefit of the
doubt than our men. We think they're definitely going to make
it. All I can say is, don't get drawn in. Don't get caught up in
the whims of others. Don't get focused on other people's problems. It's not about not caring. It's about self-preservation. You
will lose your mind trying to figure out what some people are
thinking. Girl, let the drama go. Don't let anyone add to your
stress level. Anyone stressing you or making you unhappy constantly has got to go!

The reason I say most people don't want their own happiness is because at any moment everybody has the power to
change their lives. The catalyst for changing your life lies in
your attitude. Whatever you believe will be your reality. You

are empowered each and every day to make this a life you will enjoy. You don't have to be miserable. You don't have to get caught up in day-to-day drama. You don't have to live paycheck to paycheck. Don't settle. Don't think you can't go any higher. You can have whatever you want in this life. You just have to believe and then place that belief system in action.

LESSON

Happiness is your choice. If you want it badly enough, you will find ways to achieve it.

KNOW WHO YOU ARE

———

Decide who you are
who you want to be
and then
do everything
in your power
to be that

Our situations and experiences define who we are. They define the way we feel, the way we react, what we want, and how we live.

Experiences and our reactions to them directly define our belief system. Everything you've gone through has shaped your personality. Even though you may have picked up some character traits from your family, you are unique. What you believe, what you want, what you will and will not expect, are directly linked to what you have experienced. This is your foundation in life. This is an outlook that will make or break you. It can leave you bitter or make you want to find happiness.

Life is all about what you want from it. In each and every moment you have the power to shape what you will experience. Experiences happen, but it is what we do with them that forms our character. You have the power to shape your reactions. You have the power to change your belief system. It's all about your level of thinking and whether you will let yourself take charge.

Take control of your life or you will let life control you. Know who you are and realize that at all times your destiny is in your control.

LESSON

Your foundation lies in knowing who you are and consists of your beliefs, values, and the culmination of your experiences. It will guide you in life. If your foundation is strong, you will make wise decisions. Once you are comfortable with who you are, no one can define or tell you what to do with your life. You will realize that knowing who you are and loving yourself are the keys to controlling the happiness of your life.

LOVE YOURSELF

MY WISH

In a world of mixture
I never know how my life will turn
what is true one minute
can soon become part of
a web of chaotic lies
the pure
polluted
the divine
questionable
or is it that life is scary
like a goldfish in the ocean
I swim constantly
sometimes upstream
sometimes in water as peaceful
as the Nile
I never know physically
where I will end up
but spiritually I've been
in heaven for many years
as my life goes on now
I hope out of all

in this world

at least one

true person

will remain in my life

I surely will smile

when someone can look me in the eye

and say I know you

and finally I can believe them

A TRUE FRIEND

Friendship can be a difficult thing. You think because you've known someone for so long, that they always have your best interest at heart. Sometimes, though, they only have their own interest in mind. Your personal responsibility is to make sure that the friends you have in your life are really your friends. Ask yourself: Will these people be there for me through every up and down? Do they have my back? If I really need help, would they be there?

It's very easy for us to hang out and party with one another. But when the chips are down and stuff is rough, only a few people are there for you. I remember when my father told me: "You have to be careful with those you consider friends." I thought he was crazy. Now I know that friends are extensions of you. They are your family. They are supportive. They love you no matter what. They will be there for you to tell you when you're doing good and when you're doing bad. A true friend will keep it real with you. He or she will not want anything from you but your time. She will not steal your energy or be demanding, but will be reliable.

Hanging out with your girls is cool, but there will come a time when you're going to need a support system. The best thing you can do for yourself today is know who you can depend on and who you cannot. Once you know, it's on you to either cut people loose or keep dealing with flaky friends.

LESSON

A true friend feels like family. You love and encourage each other. A true friend will push you to be the best person you can be by always encouraging you and giving you the real deal about yourself. When you're with a true friend you will feel totally comfortable.

DON'T TRY ME

—

Don't try to bend
or sway me
I stand still
in my truth
I look for answers
within myself
I have the power of God
within this body
your words cannot move me
unless they speak pure truth
that which is right for me

Don't try to bend
or sway me
I can listen
but I will not change
unless it is in my destiny
leave your foolish thoughts
and attempts to manipulate
right there
I am a partner with God

I can hear

I can feel

I can see

when you are not right

for me

I know when you are trying to persuade me

to do what's right for you

and wrong for me

Don't try to bend

or sway me

I am too powerful for this

I know myself

and I am in love

with me

therefore I do what's right

for me

STICK TO YOUR VALUES

———

At any moment you know what is right for you. But it's easy to get caught up in the moment and forget. Make sure that no man talks you out of or into any situation you don't want to be in. Realize the motivation behind other people's actions. Not everyone is looking out for your best interests. So what you have to do is remember that this is your world. There is no one in this world better than you. There is no one who knows you better than you. Therefore you're in control. You decide what is and is not acceptable. You make sure that the values your parents instilled in you do not get diminished.

LESSON

Your values are your guide to life. They will help you make the right choices, if you remember them. Always know what you want out of life. Accept no limitations and go for it.

TAKING RESPONSIBILITY

———

Don't sit comfortably
thinking you know everything
life has twists and turns
that you must be prepared for
before you do anything
think of where
it will leave you
years from now

Every simple decision will have a profound impact on your life. This means that everything you decide to do will affect the outcome of your life. You have to think before you make choices. Don't act on impulse. Know when to separate your emotions from facts and make a decision based on the facts. Many times, as women, we want to think with our hearts. But our hearts and our inner voices are not always on the same page. Your heart will keep you in some crazy situations. Your inner voice will always let you know when you need to get up and out.

Don't ever assume that someone else will cover your responsibilities for you. This is your life. Every decision you make will affect your life. It's your responsibility. People will be there for you, but don't expect more from them than you expect from or can give yourself.

Always think realistically. The worst mistake is to get caught up in the moment. You have to know when to take a step back and think. Always think about what's in your best interests.

Life is not meant to be a series of challenges that leave you feeling defeated. It is, however, meant to shape your character. I remember people always telling me: "God never gives us more than we can handle." At the time I thought, Well, maybe he doesn't know me that well. It's easy to think that way when times are really hard. But you can't give up. Look at the role you played in shaping your life. I advise you to look at your life and think before you make any choices or decisions. Think, because your life depends on it.

LESSON

The decisions we make each and every day define our responsibilities. Therefore, before we make any choice or decision, we have to think about the impact we will be making on our lives.

EXPERIENCE

———

Experience strengthens the soul
but does it harden the love
does betrayal
turn you inside yourself
until you run through
your own
mind
in search of truth
honesty
and hope
where does the love go
when experience
has hardened your innocent soul
and makes you mistrusting of others
suspicious of all

OPENING UP TO LOVE AFTER BEING HURT

The worst thing you can do is keep yourself in an endless cycle of relationships. You have to take a breather between relationships. That time in between is necessary to let go of any anger and release the baggage. No one, besides a therapist, wants to deal with you and your problems.

If a relationship even has a tinge of "I'll get you through this," it is fated to fail because it will be based on neediness. He'll need to help you. You'll need to be helped. You'll hurt him with your words and actions. He'll stick it through because "he loves you." He'll start hurting you. You'll stick with him because "you love him." And it becomes one vicious mess that you could have avoided.

You are fully empowered to take a break between relationships. It's like a breath of fresh air for your spirit. You get in tune with yourself so you don't become jaded, disillusioned, or embittered. If a man has hurt you in any way in a relationship, do not immediately enter another relationship. Do not even begin to fool yourself and say it's just sexual. That's just a relationship diversion. You have to deal with yourself before you can give yourself, in any capacity, to anyone.

It's best to know why and what you want from a relationship. Don't try to replace the last man with a new man. Don't try to hurt anyone because you've been hurt. Don't become bitter because the last man was a jerk. What you perceive will become your reality. If, based on your experiences, you think all men are jerks and ain't about nothing, guess what type of men you're going to meet. Your perception is your reality.

This is not to say that all relationships end so badly that you need time to heal. But even when one ends well you still need to take time for yourself. Comparing your new man to your ex is just as bad as being bitter—it will ruin the relationship eventually. So always take time for yourself before dating or entering new relationships.

Once you have allowed yourself to heal and you're no longer thinking about your ex or comparing other men to him, then you can consider dating. But always go into a relationship fresh. Leave behind the baggage and don't expect the new man to be a jerk or a dog.

Expect the best treatment. Expect the best relationship. Don't become intimate immediately and don't start thinking this is the one. Get to know the man you're dealing with. Get to know him as your friend. Learn how to trust. Learn how to love. But do it slowly. Don't rush. A solid relationship needs a foundation of friendship, trust, respect, honesty, and love. It takes time to develop those qualities in each other.

You can open yourself up to love, but know that love must be reciprocal. You will love him and he will love you. You will not need each other, but you will want each other. Love is not needy. Love is not possessive. Love is something that makes your life better and makes you feel happy.

LESSON

Take a breather between each relationship to renew your spirit. It will give you time to know yourself and empower you to make better choices in relationships.

THE WAY WE LEARN

A simple message

in the bottle of your soul

is opened and revealed

by anyone around you

be aware

hear the words

learn what you must

and move on

but always know

that lessons

are the fabric of your soul

and must be returned to you

one

by precious

one

to make you whole

LEARN FROM YOUR EXPERIENCES

A sign of wisdom is being able to look back on an experience and find the lesson in it. Life is not always what you dream about. There may be some obstacles along the way, some experiences that hurt you and bring you down. The way you react to your experiences is the deciding factor in how you continue to live your life.

Tao Te Ching, a spiritual book I highly recommend, states that when life becomes difficult, the weak man falls down on himself and bemoans his fate, while the strong man sees it as a challenge, a learning experience, and perseveres. Life is not about giving in to what happens and telling yourself, "This is it, this is all I will become."

Always remain in control of your life. By learning the lesson in every situation, you are remaining in control of your life.

Lessons are everywhere. To see them, you have to open your eyes. You won't see the lesson when you're in the middle of a situation. You will wonder, Why me? But, for the sake of your sanity and the advancement of your life, you need to stand back from a situation to see what's up. What was the situation supposed to teach you? Whether good or bad, there was a lesson. Also, remember that everything happens for a reason. Yes, everything. So look at your life. See the patterns. Learn from your past decisions and make better choices in the future.

If you do not look for the lesson in your situations, you are, in essence, closing your eyes to your life. You are no longer in a position to change your life. You don't have to make the same mistakes. You don't have to be stuck in any situation. You just have to be willing to learn from your mistakes and, if you are wise, you will look at the mistakes your friends have made and learn from their choices as well.

If you choose not to learn a lesson the first time, you will repeat it. Don't think you won't.

Life is about going to the next level in every endeavor. Learn from your life and make it an example to others. God gave you this life and the chance to learn. The purpose of this process, learning lessons, is for the evolution of your spirit. You do not want to waste time by continually repeating lessons, because your spirit wants and needs to continuously move forward and learn something new. You have to push yourself to the next level. Control your destiny and your spiritual evolution.

LESSON

There are lessons we all must learn in life. The way we control our lives is by opening our eyes to lessons and making the right choices.

THE ART OF THE GAME

———

If I close my eyes
because I don't want to see
but only welcome the darkness
is that a sanctuary?

If I open my eyes
and swallow the fear
follow through
even on shaky legs
does that make me courageous?

Though I may walk
with tears in my eyes
because I am afraid
of where the path leads
am I not brave
for at least walking?

If I say, There
there is my destiny
and I stand still

and point
aren't I a fool?

The art
of the game
is embracing the fear
tucking the doubt
under your arm
running
and willing your way
to personal freedom

BE OPEN TO OPPORTUNITIES

———

Don't limit your life based on what others around you have achieved. Look at life as something that you can create. Explore life. Don't limit yourself to one thing. Learn new things. Look for any opportunity to learn or do something new. Never get caught up in the same day-to-day stuff. Life is not about redundancy, it is about pushing yourself to the next level and learning. Every situation has the opportunity to teach you something about yourself and others. It's up to you to put yourself in the position to learn. You have to extend yourself and reach into life.

Every person who is caught up in day-to-day drama or who doesn't love life is afraid of risk. You have to take risks to push yourself to the next level and get more out of life. You have to always want more. Not to want more materially, but to always want to learn more. If you are not taking risks, you are not living life.

LESSON

Life is full of opportunities. Learn to embrace them and allow any fear to push you forward. It is your life to create.

THE LOWEST MOMENT IS THE BEST MOMENT

In your lowest moment

at your hardest time

your spirit struggling

your will tested

you are being created

If you allow it

and open your heart

to the lesson

your true spirit will emerge

your soul will be

your guide in life

and you will find that God never left you

he was only giving you a mirror

into your inner soul

to find how you will define your life

and whether your experiences will make

or break you

The lesson in life is that

God is always with you,

within you
in your heart
and in the way you express yourself

God is your soul

Your soul is part of God

Once you know this fully and completely
you can create the life you want
and handle any adversity

DO NOT GIVE UP ON YOURSELF

Many times we can be our own worst critic. When something goes wrong in our lives, it is easy to put ourselves down and condemn ourselves as failures. You're never a failure as long as you try to recognize the mistakes you have made and learn from them. This will help you to make better decisions in the future.

Once you have learned that you will make mistakes and can learn from them, you have no reason to ever give up on yourself. This is your life and at any moment you have the opportunity to make it what you want.

Giving up on yourself hurts your spirit. It can cause stress, depression, anxiety, and doubt. It can hinder you from exploring new opportunities. It can cause you to stay in terrible situations and accept things you never should. Don't ever do this to yourself. You are always in control. You just have to ask yourself, "Okay, this didn't work; now what can I do?"

Stay in control of your life. Stress and giving up on yourself will kill you, literally and spiritually.

Always know that you can have more out of life. You don't have to limit yourself. You don't have to be afraid. You can achieve what you want.

You are not a failure. You are human and we all experience failures and mistakes. You just have to get up and keep going. Keep living life.

LESSON

Giving up on yourself kills your spirit and can make your life become stagnant.

MY LOVE

———

If I have
If I have
If I have
everything
except you
I have nothing

You are my love
my world
I want to share this
with you
I need to have you

You are what I want
in my life
you make all this complete
then it's real
then there's happiness
then I have everything

KNOW YOUR DEFINITION
OF SUCCESS

———

Success is an inner fulfillment. It is not money or a beautiful home. You are successful when you are constantly learning, growing, allowing yourself to be open to love, and sharing that love. Success is not about status; it is about reaching your goals.

It is best to know early in life how you define success. It varies for people. For many, a certain income level defines their success. But try to go deeper than that. Money does allow you to do things that can make you happy. But you should not love money. Money is a means to a materialistic end. Never focus your love on money. Focus on the opportunities you can have and give to others through money.

Don't define success as a beautiful home or car. These are also just material things. They are not permanent fixtures. If you allow them to define who you are, then your definition will be shallow. Look beyond what a car says about you and get a car because you like it. The same is true for your choice in a home—it is a reflection of you, but it does not define who you are. You define who you are and therefore you must define what success means to you.

Success is not a permanent state. All your life you must continually set and work to attain your goals. Always push your "success" to the next level.

LESSON

Success is an inner fulfillment. It is not based on the material or physical. It is about reaching a level of comfort where you love yourself and are happy with yourself.

LIVE IN LOVE

HEALING A BROKEN HEART

———

Love is the food
of your soul
never give up on it
you need it
for your spirit to breathe

You can get through this. I know it feels painful—as though your heart's been pulled out of your mouth. But tell yourself, "I can get through this." Repeat it as often as you need to. Say it until you believe it. "I can get through this."

When love ends, we can feel confused and hurt. We can feel as if we'll never love again. We can feel like "the one" just got away. But true love does not get away from you. True love is there when you need it, when you are ready for it. So realize that although you loved someone, you have to let him go so that your true love can enter.

Don't do foolish things when you're in pain. Don't try to make him hurt the way he hurt you. Just let it go. I know it sounds simple. I know your heart is in pain. But if you want to deal with this, you're going to have to think realistically. You're going to have to pay attention to the reasons why the relation-ship ended. You're going to have to think about the part you played in the breakup. Analyze the relationship. See what lesson you can learn from it.

Even when I felt like my heart was breaking, I stopped and told myself, "I was supposed to learn this. He was supposed to teach me this." No, it didn't make me feel that much better, but it helped me to learn my lesson, and that was the ultimate point.

Everything happens for a reason. If a relationship is ending, let it end. Sometimes fighting is just delaying the inevitable. Sometimes you will just bring yourself more pain if you don't let go. Know when it's time to take a breath and let go.

LESSON

You can mend your heart. You can get through any pain. Just relax, feel the hurt, and take as much time as you need to get over it. You will get through this and things will get better if you learn your lesson and apply it in the next relationship.

A LITTLE APPRECIATION

———

When you say thank you
it makes me smile
I know then
that you realize
that I took my time
invested my energy
in you
you know
to get some more
of me
you always have to say
thank you for that
I appreciate it

SHOW PEOPLE THAT YOU APPRECIATE THEM

It is very easy to take others for granted. We become used to them being a part of our lives and doing things for us. We have to know that people are in our lives because they choose to be. They do things for us because that is their choice. Even your parents have a choice in how much they will do for you. You have to remember that everyone in your life who does things for you should be appreciated.

Say thank you when things are done for you. Even in life when it seems that things are coincidentally working out for you, say thank you to God. There is always someone or something working for your best interests. The more open you are to saying thank you and appreciating the time and energy others give for you, the more you will receive out of life.

Appreciation is a form of reciprocating love. When you can appreciate the people and events in your life, you will realize the beauty in the world and within others, and you will notice that life goes more smoothly.

Showing your appreciation is a simple act that you can perform every day; it will greatly affect your life and the lives of others for the better.

LESSON

Showing your appreciation to and for others will greatly affect your outlook on life.

KARMA

———

Queen

or king

peasant

or pawn

treat me

as you would want to be regarded

because whether I do it or not

it will come back to you

when you least expect it

and break you down

or lift you up

TREAT OTHERS AS YOU WOULD WANT TO BE TREATED

———

Now, this sounds like something we all would believe. However, if you keep it real with yourself, you know that you don't always treat others as you would want to be treated. We get caught up in our day, our mood, ourselves—and then take it out on others. It's easy to spread your cheer when you're in a good mood. But when you're in a bad mood, are you spreading that too?

We have to be mindful of the feelings of others. If we all took just one moment and thought of the other person, this would be a much better world. Consideration goes a long way in the scheme of things.

If you take a moment to think of the feelings of someone else before you react, you will shape that experience. How you respond and treat others gives you the power to control your day.

If you treat others as you would want to be treated, you will be rewarded. You'll be rewarded with better relationships, friendships, and, basically, a better life.

LESSON

Treat others as you would want to be treated, and you will be rewarded with better relationships.

ALWAYS WONDERED

Always wondered
how a woman could say
my man loves me
when she doesn't know where he goes
at night

Always wondered
how love could be believed
when people are sneaking
and deceiving

Always wondered
how things were right
as long as he was there
to pay the bills
is it all right to be smacked
long as he sticks around
and pays the rent

I'm wondering when it became all right
to receive black eyes
and be dragged
by the throat
are these loving hands

the father of your child
green keeps these people together
green love for each other

I'm wondering when you became dependent
on men who beat you
cheat on you
and lie to you
many a person has said
you are worth more
wondering if there are marbles in your head

I want to scream out loud
when I see you
no longer covering those eyes
raccoon style is now your badge
of honor
where is life headed
when you no longer feel ashamed
signs of love do not beat your side
pain your heart
or make you cry all night

I'm wondering why
it hurts me
more than
it seems to hurt you

ABUSIVE RELATIONSHIPS

In a perfect world, I would not even have to mention mental or physical abuse. But every day there are women getting beaten down and staying in the relationship.

I have to emphasize to you that the way you think about yourself directly affects what you expect and will receive in relationships. On the surface you may appear to have it all together, but only women with insecurities and low self-esteem stay in bad situations. And if they're trying to rationalize it, they're giving fear power over their life, rather than realizing that God wants them to love their life.

If a man hits you even once, he will hit you again. Never let any man think he can get away with that. Yes, he may have more strength than you, but everyone has to sleep.

It's really painful to see a woman put herself through this torture. There is nothing that should keep anyone in this type of relationship. Don't second-guess yourself. A relationship is not worth saving to "keep the family together" or because of finances. You will eventually end up without a shred of self-esteem and it will take years to rebuild it. It's simply not worth it.

There is always someone to turn to, someplace to go.

I have never been in this type of relationship and never will. But I have seen it firsthand. I have seen how a grown woman can feel like a child in her own home, afraid to speak, afraid to leave her room. I have seen the scars and the tears. I have seen the damage done in a room of "love" after a man has beaten a woman. I have heard what it sounds like. It's worse than any nightmare. It's hell.

Don't put yourself in this situation. There are always early warning signs. You'll notice when a brother is a little too possessive. It is not even remotely cute for a brother to want to know where you are every minute of the day. It's none of his business. Realize that when a brother tries to change the way you dress or pick out your clothes, he is trying to change you. He is trying to mold you into what he wants. You cannot allow this to happen. Stay true to you.

I would strongly caution against being with someone who admitted he beat a girlfriend who had pushed him to it in the past. That's not acceptable. This brother has no control over his emotions and will simply pull you into his world with his irrationality. Don't even finish the conversation. Get out of there and never look back.

Now, there are also brothers who do not hit, but put you down with words. They are attempting to break your spirit because they themselves have no strength, no inner spirit. You must never allow anyone to disrespect you in any way. This even happens in marriages because the woman believes that the husband knows her well. There is not a man in this world who knows you well enough to cut you down to shreds.

Any man who tries to rationalize his disrespect toward you is a waste of your life and your time. Don't listen to his crap, because even if you shrug it off initially, it will stick in your mind and you will come to believe his negative words. Get out while you are still sane enough to know that you are a beautiful, intelligent woman who deserves the world.

LESSON

Never allow anyone to abuse you in any way. They will kill you, either literally or spiritually.

GOOD-BYE FRIEND

———

Childhood dreams are my memories
you and I faithful friends
ever alike
now where we stand as adults
is on two different sides
you are my friend of yesteryears
a child
still exploring life with wonder
though not as a student of life
ignorance is your teacher, your friend
knowledge is my guide
how can we remain friends
on two different sides
I know you so well
you know me not at all
you stand in front of me a child
and I do not understand
I do not understand

WHEN TO END A FRIENDSHIP

As with everything in life, relationships have seasons. There are beginnings and there are endings. Sometimes friends grow apart; they no longer have anything in common and the relationship feels strained. You have to know when to end a relationship of any kind, particularly when you are no longer growing in the relationship or enjoying the other person's company.

You can feel when you are growing apart from someone. You start to just tolerate them because you have known them for so long. You listen to what they're saying only halfway and you know you're not at all interested in what they're saying. Basically, you're no longer interested in her life.

It's a hard decision, but you have to know when to say "This is it." You may not want to hurt someone's feelings, especially if you've known her since grade school or something. But you're stifling your life. When you allow yourself to listen to her conversations and go places you don't really want to go with her, you are wasting your time and therefore stifling and limiting your life. You could be out doing things you enjoy; instead you're putting yourself through needless motions.

You may not want to come right out and say this friendship is no longer working, though it is the best thing to do. You may just want to phase out talking to her on the phone. You may stop going out with her. But, if she considers you a friend, she's going to want to know why you're distancing yourself from her. The best thing you can do, initially then, is put an end to a relationship that is wasting your time. You will have to be mature and keep it real with the girl. Cut her loose and live your life. Don't try to mend something that's broken.

When you're young you think you'll be friends with your high school friends forever. Some of them will remain your friends, but you will outgrow many of them too. The best thing is to acknowledge it and move on. There are so many people in this world. You do not have to limit yourself or go through the motions just to make someone else happy.

LESSON

A progressive life is one in which you know when to end relationships that are hindering your spiritual and intellectual growth.

GO FOR YOUR HIGHEST GOAL

———

You will never have true happiness
until you do what fulfills you

Somewhere within your spirit there is something that you really want to do in this life. There is something you want to accomplish more than anything else. Sometimes, however, when you share that dream with others, they will put you down. People will tell you to be realistic. And you will push your dream to the side. I'm telling you now, don't even think of curbing your dream.

Reality is what you make it. Whatever you choose to do in this life, whatever you pursue wholeheartedly, you will achieve. You simply have to be willing to believe that it is yours to achieve. You have to know that you are meant to have the lifestyle that comes from achieving your dream. Push away the negative thinking and "realistic advice" people are pushing on you and keep moving toward your goal.

People waste time in life by constantly listening to the opinions of others. No one can tell you what to want in your life. No one can define your dream. Anything you feel strongly about is your life purpose. That means you have to fulfill it in order to live a life you love.

We all know what we want out of this life, we are just often disillusioned into thinking we cannot achieve it. You have to tune out the voices of others, listen to your heart, and work at making your highest goal your reality. If you believe it, if you want it, and are willing to work for it, you can and will achieve your goals. It just depends on how badly you want to achieve that dream. If your desire is strong, there is nothing and no one that can deter you from achieving your dream.

LESSON

The dream that you really want is what will help you achieve your spiritual purpose in life. That is the reason you are here on this earth, so you have to work toward it and live a life you love.

IT'S ALL SPIRITUAL

———

What you wish
is what you get
what you want
is what you see
train your mind
live through the spirit
and visualize life
as you want it
if you focus on that
you will see
dreams can
become reality

YOUR EXPECTATIONS
DETERMINE YOUR REALITY

———

Do you know what you're doing when you say "I can't do this"? You are limiting your life. In other words, whatever you repeat to yourself, your mind will interpret as reality. Therefore, by telling yourself you cannot do this or that, it becomes true to your mind. You've limited your capabilities by thinking a foolish thought.

Program your mind to know that you can achieve what you want, you can have what you want, you can have a life you love. How do you program your mind? You tell yourself all the things you need to hear to push yourself forward. Everything that you wish someone would say to inspire you, say to yourself. If you need to hear that you're beautiful in order to feel confident, tell yourself you're beautiful.

Be your own inspiration. You do not have to look outside for inspiration or heroes. You can do it yourself. You can look up to others, but they're not going to make you feel good about yourself. Only you can do that through what you think about and how you make that your reality.

The reason to program your mind is so you will have a strong foundation. In this life, you have to have self-confidence, self-esteem, ambition, and be determined. The only way you can possess those qualities, though, is to internally and fully believe that you are the best. If you keep telling yourself terrible things like I can't, I won't, or I never, you will doom your life to those realities. If you want to have a life in which you are happy, you have to gear yourself to the upside— the "I can achieve whatever I want, there's no one in this world better than me, I can live a life I love," type of thinking.

Think of the life you want and what it holds. Focus on those things. Because whatever you focus on, you will achieve.

LESSON

Life is what you expect to happen. Your perception and belief system will affect what you experience and what you achieve in this life.

SHAPE YOUR LIFE

THE FOUNDATION OF LOVE

———

If you don't know
you have no foundation
you cannot build
you cannot feel
you cannot experience

Find the love
that exists within you
the love that others have
for you
and realize
it is just a glimpse
of the love of the universe
the embrace of God

WHO OR WHAT IS GOD?

———

God is a spiritual being that exists within you, within others, and within the world. God is the force that created you and everything in this world. God created the world as a place for man and nature to coincide.

God is not a wrathful, vengeful being. He is not a being for you to be afraid of. God created everything in nature to work with and complement everything else. Sunsets, mountains, and the earth itself are things of beauty. A being that created all these wonderful things is not something to fear. You can have awe for the works of God. But to be fearful of God limits our relationship with Him. God is a loving being you should love.

In the same way that all things in nature complement one another, humans are also here to complement one another. That means that life is about learning and about giving. All you have to do in this life is learn about yourself and give what you know. Life is really not difficult if you look at it in the simplistic terms God has given us.

You learn in this life through your experiences. Those experiences shape your life, your character, your values, your beliefs, your goals, your love, and your reality. While you are going through your life lessons, there will be a goal you want to fulfill. This goal is your reason for being, because, while you are here to learn, you are also here to fulfill a purpose. Fulfilling that purpose is like completing an agreement with God. He gave you a desire and you have to achieve it.

When you fulfill that dream, your spiritual purpose, you are giving the most beautiful thing to the world. You are giving yourself as a completely fulfilled person. This is the reason you are here: to learn, to give, to fulfill your purpose.

Your purpose is what you most desire. Any ambition, any goal is acceptable. Whether it's to start a day care center or become an entertainment lawyer. The outcome is still the same— you are in a position to help others.

To always remember your purpose, you have to remember that God is within you. Since God is the creator, this means that you are, in a way, the cocreator of your life. You can create the life you want by simply believing you must and can achieve it. Whatever you focus on and work toward, you will achieve.

Fulfilling your purpose is a spiritual act. Spirituality is about looking within and looking at the world. The world is beautiful. You will see it if you take the time to truly look at the world. It's easy to see just the negative things and the bitter people and think of the world as ugly. But the world becomes ugly because people don't realize that they are the cocreators of their lives. No one has to remain miserable or unhappy, it's all a choice.

Really look at the world, the trees, the oceans, the mountains. All of it is beautiful and designed for a specific purpose. Everything automatically works well together. Your responsibility is to fulfill your purpose so that, in some way, you contribute to how the world works too.

One person can make a difference, and that is what you are here to do. If you touch the life of one person, you are creating a domino effect. That person will touch the life of another person, and so on. So always know that you fulfilling your purpose is necessary to the world.

LESSON

God is within you and therefore you have the power to create the life you want. When you create the life you want, your inner fulfillment and happiness will be passed on to others as an inspiration.

BEAUTIFUL LOVE

Did you ever love someone
so much
that it feels like a dream
just too good to be true
but so strong you can't deny

You want to show him
that you love him
you appreciate him
you adore him
in every way

A love that makes you feel all aglow
just by
the thought of him

His words are gold
like nectar to your soul
inspiring you
touching you
in just the right way

A love that seems like a gift
because no one can be better than this
and you know that he loves you
in the same beautiful way

THE FIRST TIME

———

Sex should always be with someone you love. Remember that you never want to do anything you'll regret. You also don't want to have sex because you got caught up in the moment or just to get it out of the way. Your first sexual experience is going to define how you feel about being intimate for the rest of your life. So, the first time, you better make sure you know what love is and that you are with someone you love.

Though I'm not that much older than you, our worlds are sometimes completely different. In my day—I know that sounds old—but, really, in my day, it was an honor to be a virgin. You felt devastated and disgusted if anyone said you weren't a virgin. You did not want to be accused of having had sex at an early age.

Now, though, you girls are acting as if being a virgin is like being called a slut. You have your morals backward. Stay a virgin until you find a man you love and you are emotionally ready for a mature relationship.

Every woman deserves a guy who treats her like gold and honors her. That's the one you want and should wait to experience this precious moment with. You want a guy who is going to appreciate that he's your first. Not because he's glad to get some. But because he really loves you and is glad you're sharing such an intimate experience with him.

I do not regret my first sexual experience. I was old enough to know I wanted to be with the guy and mature enough to know that he loved me. We still love and respect each other. That's what you want to be able to say. So choose who you want to be with wisely.

If you do decide to have sex, please use protection. You can wind up a young unhappy mother or a young woman with AIDS. I know a girl who was diagnosed as HIV-positive her first semester of college. She had only been sleeping with one guy. She still looks "normal." So don't assume any stupid crap, like you'd be able to tell if someone has it. You won't know unless a doctor diagnoses it, so use protection.

Also, if you're going to have sex, make sure you have a loving environment. I can't believe the number of women who have lost their virginity in the backseat of a car. I personally think that's unacceptable. There's no love in the backseat of a car—that's a quickie. Keep it real with yourself and make sure, again, that this is a person who loves and respects you. No man who respects or loves you would even consider having you lose your virginity in such a demeaning way.

You have to be sure that you both want to take this relationship to the next level. Sex is just another extension of a relationship. Never have sex because you think it will make a relationship better. Or "because everyone else is doing it," which is the most idiotic thing I've heard.

If you're not able to talk to your parents about protection, as many young girls aren't, see if there is someone else you can talk to about it. It's a lot better to ask for protection now than to go through an unwanted pregnancy or receive a terrible disease. So ask an aunt or family friend about it or walk your butt into the closest Planned Parenthood center.

Don't expect the stuff you see on TV. First sex is usually nothing like that, even when it's with someone you love. You'll both be a little nervous and will not really know what you're doing.

I don't think you should have sex when you're so young, because it can add complications to your life. Plus, sex is much better when you're mature and know the difference between love and infatuation. However, being realistic, I know there are many girls who are just as willing as boys to take it to another level. So just remember to share yourself with someone you genuinely love, and always use protection.

LESSON

Sex is an intimate act between a couple who loves and respects each other.

WATCH WHAT YOU SAY

———

Words

can come back

so watch

what you throw out

a little fake PMS here

can win you

B of the year

lonely and miserable

with no one to shed a tear with

watch what you throw out

say what you feel

a stack of apologies

are nothing but garbage

to the pain caused a soul

by your insensitive

foolish remarks

watch your bitterness

before it spreads

through your body

and manifests as

experience

nothing but lies
because you'd rather hide your heart
and let your mouth flow
that misery is reeking, girl
pretty soon
everyone will
run from you

DON'T SPREAD YOUR MISERY

There are many females who treat their men like crap. They yell at them and put them down. I have a friend who yelled at her man so bad in front of me, it sent chills down my spine. If a man irritates you that much, then you should strongly consider being single. Why would you be with someone whom you obviously don't respect and cannot love? If you love someone, then you care about his feelings. You care about how your words will affect him.

There's a misconception that in order to have a strong relationship, you have to keep your man in check, that what you say goes. Now, there's nothing wrong with having some control in a relationship—you don't want to be passive. But you also want to make sure that both of you have control in the relationship.

Imagine someone yelling at you, in front of your friends even, and telling you what to do and when to do it. You'd instantly kick them to the curb. Yet we expect the men in our lives to take our drama, our yelling and screaming as part of dealing with a female. What we really need is to consider their feelings as well as we consider our own. No, men are not as emotional as we are, and, yes, they can take yelling a little bit better than we can. But do they want to deal with this stuff? Oh hell, no, they don't. They will deal with it until they can't take it anymore. So watch it when you yell and get so upset that you tell your man he's stupid and whatever else comes to your mind.

A true lady treats her man with the same respect she would want. A woman knows that she doesn't have to put anyone down in order to make herself feel better.

Keep your expectations of your man realistic. If he didn't do something before he got involved with you or married you, he's not suddenly going to do it once he's with you. You have to look at the person you're with for the person he is right now. Realize that the things you think are important or essential may not be so important to your man. No one wants to hear you nag and yell. Your friends don't want to hear about how you had to nag him either. It's all just too irritating and, eventually, any man will want to get away from a nagging, miserable person as soon as he can.

LESSON

Realize that what you deem to be important or essential may not be as important to others. This does not lessen its importance, it just means that you realize the situation can be reversed. Your friend or man may find something important that you don't think matters much. But you can still respect each other and the right of each of you to determine when, what, and how you want to do things in life.

CONFIDENCE IS NOT AN ATTITUDE, IT'S A STATE OF MIND

Confidence is not an attitude
it is knowing
feeling
believing

Confidence is an assertion
a proclamation
I am the best
because I am me

I know you see people who look confident to you because of the way they walk, their faces, or their words. But confidence is not an outer attitude. It's a state of mind. There are many people out there walking the confidence walk who are really very insecure.

So while you do want to have your confidence walk, and look as if you have your stuff together, you also want to really have your stuff together—that means believing in yourself, loving yourself, and respecting yourself.

How do you believe in yourself? Your beliefs have been affected by many things in your life. Your parents, your friends, television, your family, your boyfriends, all have had a part in shaping your belief system. Whatever has been instilled in your mind has become your reality, your truth. If what you believe or have been told is positive, such as you're beautiful, you're intelligent, you can be anything you want, or you are loved, then hold on to these beliefs.

If, however, you've had a much harsher glimpse of life, and people—even your parents—have put you down, then you have to let all of that go and rebuild yourself. Their negative words can only affect you for as much or as long as you allow it. Often people put others down because they can't see life the way the other person does. Their lives have become closed. When people hurt you, it may not always be intentional—it may just be the only way they know how to relate. But that is his or her personal problem and you cannot allow it to affect you any longer.

To believe in yourself, you have to have a foundation of love, respect, and confidence within and for yourself. You have to learn how to eliminate your negative beliefs and live life in a more loving way.

To love yourself, you have to like yourself. You have to like the person you are. The person you are is shaped by the decisions you have made and what you believe. When you make any decision, base it on whether it is truly a reflection of you. When you make decisions that are a reflection of who you really are and live your life based on your truth, you become a person that you can respect and love.

LESSON

Confidence is an essential state of being. It is based on loving, respecting, and appreciating yourself. Making decisions that reflect who you are and want to be as a person will help you like and love yourself and will give you more confidence.

MY ANGEL

Angels of light
shining brightly
warming the soul
through memories
pictures of love

You are my angel now
I love you more
than I could ever say
I feel your spirit
and I thank you
for sticking with me
in this time of need
by showing me
that heaven is having peace
and sharing it

I see you every night
in the stars
I see you in the stream of light

cascading from the sun
I see you in the mirror
when I smile
I know as long as I have love for you
I have you

You are my angel
I love you

DEALING WITH DEATH

———

Death is a continuation, not an end. That means that when people die, they simply go somewhere else. Though they have left your physical world and you can't see them, they still exist. They exist in your heart and your memories. They exist in heaven. Their spirit is with God.

It's devastating as a young person to have to deal with death. While you don't think about whether you're going to die tomorrow, when someone dies you may begin to wonder if everyone around you is going to start dying. It's very scary and traumatic. The reality is that everyone is going to die. And I think parents and loved ones may try to hide that fact from you. It's not fair and it doesn't make dealing with death any easier. If anything, it just looks as if they're in denial.

Everyone does eventually pass on to be with God once again. So what you can do now is focus on the time you have with people. Live life to the fullest. Let people know you love and care about them. And always know that if someone is sick or in need, you should be there for them. It's important for both of you.

One day, my dear, you are going to pass on too. That does not mean that you give in to grief and stress and take your own life. Your life is a precious gift. You have a spiritual agreement with God to live, learn, and love here. If you are in need of someone to get you through a tough time, then reach out and ask for that help. Don't think there's no one available to help or to listen. There are many people who are very loving and willing to help.

It is painful to lose someone you love. It's hard to deal with, but remember they live on not only in your heart, but their spirit is still present, still watching over you. Now you have your own personal angel.

LESSON

Realize that death is something that will happen to everyone. Therefore you should tell and show people that you love and appreciate them while you have the chance. Live and enjoy your life completely and in such a way that you will have no regrets.

WHERE AM I GOING?

———

One, two, three, go
Go?
Go where?
You don't know?
You better find out

Oh my God
can we start again?
You're crazy
you better keep running

But where am I going?
You should have known that
before you left the gate
run girl
run

HAVE GOALS

Many women regret that they didn't make wiser choices in their lives. They feel as though they just got caught up in life—simply took whatever job was available, ended up dating whatever man asked them out. It doesn't mean they were taking crap, just that they allowed life to lead them.

If there's anything women would change about their lives, it's their focus. Looking back, they honestly would pay more attention to their education and less to the boyfriend they thought they loved to death.

It's necessary for your happiness to know what you want out of life. High school can be fun and one of the best times of your life. But once you are out of school, life is going to come at you head-on and you're going to have to know how to deal. Knowing, as they say, is half the battle. Once you know what you want, don't let anything or anyone deter you. You will come to regret it if you do. Make decisions that are right for you.

I'm going to go all out for you and admit Mom is not always right. There are many mothers and daughters who are not emotionally close. Therefore, Mom telling you what to do may not be as helpful as a friend who truly knows you. Yes, Mom wants the best for you, but if she doesn't *know* you, well, she can mislead you. You know, deep down, what's right for you.

The next step is to make a life plan. Once you know what

you want out of life, you have to plan ways and set deadlines to achieve it. Life will be so much easier for you this way. So write down your goals and write down what you need to do to accomplish them. Then base your choices on achieving those goals. Become an intern in your field. Take entry-level jobs in that area. Don't think any job is unimportant. Every job is important when you have a life plan. When you have a life plan, the jobs you choose are going to be based on getting you closer to your dream. That means instead of being a fry-cook, you take a job as a receptionist so you can learn how to deal with clients. Use your jobs to your advantage and don't get too comfortable. That's another trap.

There are many people who started jobs at young ages and never moved on to anything else. That's your parents' generation. Once they got a good job, they stayed put. Nowadays, however, times are different. People don't stay put the way they used to. And it's not something you need to make your reality anyway. You're not at a job to make friends, you're there to learn and grow. You want to have a job that challenges you and pushes you toward your goals. Don't ever get complacent and just try to stick it out. If it's not your dream job, it's just a step along the way. Definitely don't quit one job until you have another. But always keep learning new things and looking for opportunities to get closer to your goals.

Learn from the mistakes of other women as you take control of your life. Make a life plan and stick to it. Accomplish your goals. Yes, you can work toward your goals at any age. But it's so much easier when you haven't become stagnant, complacent, and you don't have overwhelming responsibilities, so that you can simply live your life.

LESSON

Take control of your life by making a life plan, listing your goals, and figuring out ways to accomplish them.

USE YOUR RESOURCES

DON'T TELL TOO MUCH
ABOUT YOUR MAN

———

If you keep saying
something is sooo good
pretty soon
someone will want to know
if it's better than what they got
and just how good
is sooo good

When we enter a relationship that is thrilling us, we feel joyful and want to share that experience. We want to tell our friends and family just how wonderful this man is. We want them to know how special and loved he makes us feel. But, as many women say, "A good man is hard to come by," and if you keep talking about yours while your friends are dealing with crap, they're either going to get jealous or distant, or want what you've got.

Every woman wants to be treated special, with respect and love. But not everyone can deal with how wonderful your relationship is if they're not currently experiencing the same thing. It is in your best interest to just hold back on the info sometimes. No one needs to know what goes on in the bedroom or what he says to you.

Also, be careful of always having your best friend and your

man around each other. Of course you want to be with both of them, but they may become cozier than you'd like.

Remember that your friends and family do want you to be happy. But to remain happy, you have to keep some of your business to yourself.

LESSON

The best relationship is one in which the partners honor the commitment and sacredness of their relationship.

KICK MR. POTENTIAL
TO THE CURB

———

When you try to pull
someone up
they can pull you down
if their will to stay
is stronger
than your desire
to rise

Kick Mr. Potential to the curb. Yes, that sounds harsh. But, Mr. Potential is the one you're saying would be a better man if ____. This is the man you like and could learn to love. This is the guy you think will someday be a decent man. This is a guy who has drama. He is a walking headache. This is not the man who is busting his butt to make something of his life. Oh no, this Mr. Potential is the whining, complaining, lazy guy who "just can't get a break." This guy is the one you run from like the wind.

Mr. Potential has had a couple of breaks in his life. He was just starting to do this when that happened. Or he was just about to make it and then, bam, somebody did that. Don't think life is going to get better for the guy now that you're there. Your friendship and/or love will not help this guy. The only person who can help him is himself. Mr. Potential has to create his own life. You can't try to make it for him. He has to get past the potential and learn how to be a man for himself, by himself.

This is one of those "do I want to be happy or do I want to survive?" moments. Life is more than survival. Go for the happiness and kick Mr. Potential with no ambition to the curb.

LESSON

You cannot (always) change the life of another with your good intentions or friendship. If someone wants to change his life, he has to want it for himself.

DON'T PUT MARRIAGE BEFORE
THE RELATIONSHIP

———

Going to the chapel
What's his name?
please
I'm about to get . . .
What's his mama's name?
I got this ring
What does he do?
I don't care
I got everything I need

Many women are so focused on an engagement ring and wedding day that they completely look past the faults of the man they're dealing with. Women seem to be under the false impression that a man will change when he gets married. If he's cheating on you now, if he doesn't cook or clean up after himself, if he doesn't like your family and they don't like him, guess what. Nothing's going to change, except your focus will be off your beautiful wedding day and on how unhappy you are with this guy who can't even wash a dish or pick up his clothes.

Initially, when dating, men show you their sweet, wonderful, considerate side. Then as they get more used to you, they let their guard down. If they are, in fact, sweet, considerate guys, they stay that way. If, however, they were just trying to make a good impression and now they're being real, take that realness as a sign from God and get out if you can't deal. Marriage is nothing but a continuation of what you already have.

Another reason not to run around telling yourself he's the one is because you still have to really get to know this brother. I don't care what he says. I don't care if he's describing your dream life when he tells you how your life together will be. Don't start looking at white dresses. Make sure the brother is not just telling you what you want to hear or what he needs to say. You have to realize that sometimes people are just talk. Look at his life. See what he's doing to make his dreams reality. Do his actions show that he's a considerate, loving, ambitious man? Or do they tell you he's a different type of person altogether? Before you fall for anyone, make sure that he has proved to you that he is worthy of your love and your time.

Also, when you're not busy deciding what carat you want, you allow a relationship to unfold. Allow the relationship to take its own course. This is very important and very necessary. When the focus is off "Is he the one?" you can focus on the friendship within the relationship. You can honestly get to know the man. You're not overlooking any flaws. You're appreciating the things he does for you. You're building a real relationship.

LESSON

Marriage is a continuation of a relationship. It should be experienced with someone you love and regard as a friend, someone that you want to grow and share your life with, someone that you love with the very essence of your being. The only way to find out if a man is that someone is to give it time. Take your eyes off the carat and look at the man. Make sure he's the right fit for your life.

AN UNCOMPLICATED LIFE

———

You cannot be the crutch
if there is no will to stand

You cannot be the life
if there is no desire to live

You cannot be the love
if the heart is closed

You cannot be the dream maker
if there are no wishes to fulfill

You cannot be everything
you cannot be anything
to someone
who doesn't want
an uncomplicated life

DON'T TRY TO COMPENSATE FOR YOUR MAN'S HARD-KNOCK LIFE

———

There are so many talented, beautiful women who get caught up in the drama of their men's lives. If a man is experiencing drama when you meet him and you continue to date him, you're asking for trouble. If he's just getting over drama, you're asking for trouble. This is not to say that men have to go through things in life alone. Rather, it means that women tend to try to compensate for their men.

Every sister who is struggling with a man, pretty much, will tell you he had a hard life. His family situation was terrible; they just didn't treat him right. They still don't treat him right. It's like he's not part of the family. You know what I say? Boo-hoo. This man, this relationship, will kill your spirit. Eventually you won't know what happened to your life because the years have passed you by.

There is no amount of love or friendship that can make up for the traumas this guy has experienced. Your love cannot substitute for the therapist and counselor he so desperately needs. You are not the owner of his problems. You should not try to be his one good friend or example of a loving family. You are just pulling yourself into some avoidable drama.

You have to realize that no one has a perfect family life. And the number of women who deal with or have experienced child abuse, domestic violence, infidelity, etc., is astronomical. But still we persevere. We get up every day and go through life. We find jobs. We find rides. We find day care. We find a way. A real man would do the same thing.

For your own peace of mind and a better life, allow this man to find his own strength. Allow him to find his way. And never try to compensate for the issues a guy has been dealing with for years. You will only hurt yourself and encourage him to become dependent and needy.

This is a stifling, unhappy relationship that has no positive outcome. The only result will be a miserable, struggle-filled life.

LESSON

You cannot compensate for the hard life of another person by trying to be his everything. People need a chance to heal without using another person as a crutch.

DON'T JUDGE OR LIMIT YOURSELF BY THE THOUGHTS OF OTHERS

———

While you have a right
to your opinions and such
I am the only one
who can define me
so your opinions
don't matter much

It's easy to fall into the trap and believe the limiting things people say about us. It is easy to think, Well, maybe they're right. But this line of thinking gives people power over your life. They are defining your life and what you will become. You never want to give anyone power over your life. You have to disregard whatever anyone says about you and believe in yourself.

Sometimes you literally have to stop yourself in your life and say: "This is it. This is my life. I define it. I live it. I control it." Then you have to make decisions for yourself. Wherever you focus your energy, you focus your time. You cannot waste mental energy or time focusing on what others think of you.

Even loved ones will try to tell you what to do with your life. Thank them for their opinion, then make your own decision. No one who constantly allows her life to be directed by others will ever lead a happy life.

Don't give in to the shapers of society. Don't think you have to be thin, look a certain way, or have to wear a certain label. Be your own person. Be original. Love the way you are.

LESSON

Never allow others to define your life, because then they will control you.

THIS LITTLE LIGHT

———

There is no love
better than this
the person
who kisses my soul
shares my dreams
wants a life
with me
this man I love
who loves me
does not rush me
as we fulfill our dreams
we will see
when the time is right
for our souls to meet
and bring that light
into the world

HAVE CHILDREN WHEN YOU ARE READY, NOT BECAUSE YOU LOVE SOME MAN

———

As women, it is easy to feel that we are in love with or love a man. We feel that if he treats us right, respects us, and is there for us, then we can give him our all. Usually we can. But there are always those instances when a woman didn't take enough time to get to know the man she was dealing with. Either she became intimate or she thought she was in love too early in the relationship.

Relationships need time to develop. And we cannot give in to our hearts so quickly that we don't know deep down if this is "the one." I personally thought I had met a great person. He was loving and considerate. And then things changed. The relationship changed. And I was left in a situation I never expected. I was a single parent.

There is no amount of preparation that can help you with being a single parent. It is difficult. It is challenging. It will change your life.

If you don't want to end up in the same situation, then get to know the guy you're dealing with. Don't become intimate too soon. Wait until you really know the person. Know that you love him. Know that you want to spend the rest of your life with him. And that the feelings are reciprocated.

A friend suggested that I include this topic in the book.

When he first said it, it felt like a slap in the face. It was as if he was saying: "Tasha, why didn't you think before you had children with this guy?" And I felt terrible because I had thought about it. I didn't just rush into a relationship. I didn't tell myself he was the one. But I confused those feelings of infatuation with love. And then I had sex early in the relationship. A cycle began because I became pregnant and then I felt stuck. I wasn't supposed to be a single parent, so I became intent on making the relationship work. I felt it was my obligation to give my children a family. My main motivation was to make sure my daughters had their father in their lives.

The one thing I do remember, though, is that I ignored my intuition. I remember, so clearly now, my intuition telling me, "This isn't the one." I chose to ignore that little voice and continue with the relationship because he was a sweet guy. He was a sweet guy, but he wasn't the one. And now I'm something I never wanted to be, a single parent.

My advice to you is to know the difference between love and infatuation. Know if your man is someone you can depend on. Know if he is someone who has dreams, goals, and plans. Know if he has a decent relationship with his family. Know that he doesn't use drugs of any kind. Know what you are getting yourself into when you begin a relationship with him. Know that the relationship is as important to him as it is to you. Know him well. Then get to know him some more. Spend time with him and share life with him until you know that you love each other fully and completely.

LESSON

Make sure that you have taken the time to live your life and accomplish some of your goals. Have a child when you are emotionally, financially, spiritually, mentally, and physically ready. It will be much more rewarding to share life with a man you love and the embodiment of that love, your children, together.

KEEP YOUR FREEDOM

WHY?

Why are we born

to those we despise

why are we born

to those we dislike

why are we born to the unsympathetic

the uncaring

the unkind

why are we born

to the show-ers

of public adoration

who give private hell

why are we born

only to be forgotten

and left in the hands of the law

why are we born

to the sniffers of coke

smokers of crack

why are we born

to die of their disease

where is our strength

where is our chance

why are we born
to those with no hope
who have no future
thus ending ours
why are we born
to live in the torture
of the perpetual question
why

RELEASE YOUR HATRED, FORGIVE OTHERS

———

The force that affects us the most throughout our lives is our emotions. Our life is shaped by what we feel and how we perceive things. Though we can remember good and bad moments, it is focusing on the bad moments—the painful times—that can have a seriously negative effect on our lives.

There are many reasons why people harbor anger in their hearts. Many mothers do not realize the power their words have over their children. A mother can define her child's life through her words of encouragement or anger. It is this that her children remember. It is what mothers believe about their children that will shape their lives.

Many times the difference between a so-called failure and a success is the relationship someone had with her mother. I know this from looking at everyday situations and seeing how people deal with and respond to their mothers. A child who has been verbally hurt by his mother or father will never forget it. That child will remember the pain of those words. The pain will turn into anger as the child approaches adulthood and comes to understand the effect the parents had on his or her life.

Another common, but often unspoken, reason we hold on to anger is if we ever dealt with sexual abuse in our lives. A child whose childhood was interrupted by some disgusting person will never forget it. And if the molester was a parent or relative, the pain goes even deeper.

It is devastating to have these types of experiences thrown at you, especially when you're a child. You are defenseless and being taken advantage of. But, for your psychological well-being and the freeing of your soul, you will have to release the pain as an adult.

Begin forgiving by releasing the anger, releasing the pain, and let the person deal with what they did to you. Whatever anyone has ever done to you is not significant enough to affect your life anymore. You have to let it go. The pain, the anger, the hurt, the fears, everything, has to go so that you can move on with your life. So that you can love again. And trust again. You have to do it. Just as you cannot allow anyone to define your life, you cannot allow anyone to cripple it, either through your fear or anger. It's simply not worth it. Your life is meant to be much more than this.

You are only hurting and hindering yourself by holding on to anger and pain. Take your power back. Begin again by releasing the hatred and anger and live this life for yourself.

LESSON

If you do not forgive, you will not grow. If you do not release hatred from your heart, you will close yourself off from the beauty and enjoyment of life and love.

ACTIONS ARE LOUDER
THAN WORDS

———

Actions are louder than words

so although your mouth is moving

I ain't really hearing nothing

I've learned to tune out

whatever you spew

and stand back

to see what you do

your mouth is like quicksand

being drowned out

'cause you're talking

but you ain't saying nothing

your mind is not moving

your body is not moving

you are stagnant

and getting on my nerves

Actions are louder than words

Actions

are louder

than words

Hear me?

DON'T COMPLAIN IF YOU ARE NOT WILLING TO CHANGE

———

There are countless women who complain about the state of their relationships and the state of their lives, but they never do anything to change it. They will tell you how they need to go back to school. How they need to leave a man. How they need to do this and they need to do that. When the one thing they need to do is to stop moaning and start moving.

No one wants to hear you say I'm going to do this and then watch as you do nothing. Not a true friend, anyway. A true friend wants the best for you, especially your happiness. If life is stagnant or a relationship is dead, get out, move on. Sounds too simple? It isn't. You just say this is enough, I'm out, and you leave.

The only thing holding these women back is themselves. They're blocking their own happiness. They're holding back their lives by sitting there talking and complaining. If you want so much out of life, if you want more, you're going to have to work for it. You're going to have to go for it. When your mouth is moving and your body's not, you're just wasting time. The years will pass by and you will still be saying, "My life shouldn't be like this." When all along you have the power to make life anything you want.

LESSON

Actions speak louder than words.

THE ESSENCE OF KINDNESS

When it is truly felt

it is mine to give

how much or how little

it is my decision

based on what I feel I can

it is my desire to do more

not because of what you think

but because my soul cries

at the heartache of others

my spirit feels the pain

my heart remembers the loss

I am not too far from you

for I am human

and life has many changes

this was not planned

this was not planned

this was not planned

but maybe my one deed

that one smile

can help

to make you see

that life can always change

and people do care

LET YOUR GOOD DEED SPEAK FOR ITSELF

———

Nothing takes away from an act of kindness more than a person who continually tells others about it. If, in fact, what you did was from your heart, you do not have to and would not want to impress others with it. Sure, there are times when you have strong feelings about something, so you tell your girls about it. But I'm talking about situations when you're really just saying: "Look at me, look at what a good person I am."

Your heart speaks for you. You do not have to tell others what type of person you are. Your actions and character will speak for you. Do things that express your individuality and your love of humanity. Don't do things just to impress others. Don't do things just because it is the "thing" to do. Do what feels right for you and leave it at that.

A little humility at the right time and in the right situation will lead you to continue to do great acts and will allow those you help to appreciate your loving spirit.

LESSON

An act of kindness should be an expression of your spirit and not intended to impress.

DECISION

Like the blades of grass
that make up the lawn
we are each a part
of life
and each distinct

It is a choice
to decide which way we will go
what turn we will make in life
the eternity of our lives
depends on our spirit
the connection we have made
the love we hold within

DESIGN YOUR LIFE

———

Everything in your life should be a reflection of you. It should consist of the person you are and wish to be. Your friends should be an extension of you and able to help you grow. Every relationship in your life should be healthy, loving, and supportive.

Many times we hold on to things for comfort. We're just used to someone or a certain situation. We have to know when to break the complacency and go on to the next level. There are levels in life and therefore levels in friendship. Every friendship is not going to last until your dying day. You have to know when a relationship is not beneficial to you.

If you have a friend that you know would not be there for you in hard times, but you remain friends with her, you are limiting yourself. You are saying that your relationships don't have to offer you anything, that you are willing to accept someone who just likes you rather than having a friend who loves and supports you no matter what. You are instilling a belief in people and yourself that others don't have to give to you. You are telling people you don't expect much, that way no one has to go out of their way or do anything extraordinary to please you.

By limiting yourself to these types of friendships, you are affecting your whole life. You're keeping yourself from experiencing relationships based on friendship, honesty, trust, and love. If these components aren't part of a relationship, you don't have a friendship and you certainly can't have a romance.

You cannot allow yourself to excuse the behavior of others. Just being aware of a situation does nothing. You have to both be aware and eliminate the "friendship." Stop putting your life on hold by dealing with people who do not have your total best interest at heart. Obviously they do not love you. Surround yourself with a family of friends who love and support you.

When you decide whom you will or will not spend time with and befriend, you gain control in other parts of your life as well. You will see that you will start to make better choices based on what's right for you. You will team up with people who have your interest and theirs in mind. Life won't seem like such a struggle when you surround yourself with people you know you can depend on.

LESSON

Knowing deep down that there are people who will be there for you because they care about you enables you to be more confident in all parts of your life.

BE YOURSELF

LOVING MYSELF

If I have me

in full

and believe

in myself

I do not have to question

you

I do not care

I do not define

my life

based on you

because I am glorious

my God

I am me

RESPECT IS A SIMPLE THING

———

Many of you young girls walk around thinking you know what respect is. But I think you have been misinformed. Respect is not about disrespecting others. Respect is not about thinking others are inferior to you. Respect is an inner belief based on loving yourself and having confidence. When you believe in yourself, no one else can affect you. You do not compare yourself to others or put them down. You are happy with who you are and what you are capable of doing.

Respect is a simple thing. Give it and you will get it.

Respect is knowing *I can, I will, I must, I am,* about yourself and not allowing anyone's opinion to sway you. When you have respect for yourself, you realize that other people are important too. With self-respect, you open your life to challenges, opportunities, and learning experiences.

LESSON

Respect is something you will receive when you are willing to give it.

SISTER KNOW EVERYTHING

———

Choking

choking

choking

on your words

you're stuffing them down my throat

faster than I can swallow

a breath is needed

but you're not giving

you believe the stuff you're saying

without even stopping

or breathing

or listening

what is going on here

who is this woman

who thinks she knows

me

the world

everything

everyone

belittling

but really putting herself down

by closing herself up

in her own world

where she is queen

and no one else exists

and no one else wants to

they just look away

and from afar say

that girl

is a fool

PUSHINESS IS NOT BEAUTIFUL

———

There are many women who feel they challenge men when they speak their mind. Speaking your mind is in no way a bad thing. It is the way that you speak that can be the problem. You may need to understand that not everyone is intimidated by your aggressive and assertive behavior. You may just be working someone's last nerve.

A woman who thinks she knows everything yet does not open herself to learning from others is a nuisance. There is no one in this world who knows everything. Each and every day of your life you should be learning—every day. So instead of thinking you're being a challenge, close your mouth and listen for a while. You just may learn something.

When you don't listen, no one will listen to you. When you are not open to learning from those you debate with, they will not try to hear what you say either.

To get the most out of life, you have to realize that it is a learning experience. That means that at any moment, at any time, you can learn something that will change your life. Anyone can teach you something valuable, you just have to be willing to learn.

LESSON

Those who are always seeking to challenge and debate close their lives to listening and learning from others and will remain stagnant until they learn that everyone is a teacher.

NO REGRETS

I never want to say

I wish

oh I wish

never want to say

I would have

I would have

I could have

really should have

I never want to say these things

never want to feel that pain

see the look of disappointment

on my own face

feel the tears glide down

as I realize the years have escaped

oh no

I can't do that to myself

my heart

would never forget

the pain

the life

the time

that was wasted

LIVE YOUR LIFE
WITHOUT REGRET

The last thing you want to do in life is look back and regret the choices you did or did not make. There is no way to go back, no way to correct life. Once a choice is made, it usually has lasting effects. So look clearly at your life and where you want to be, and make decisions that will get you the most out of life.

It is very painful to look back on life and wish you had done this or that. It's something I vowed I would never do to myself. I advise you to make the same vow and stick to it. This vow is not simple. Realize that when you vow never to regret, you are affirming that you will do something with your life, you will live life to the fullest, you will make decisions that enrich your life, and you will always try new things. You are making a commitment to yourself to try to create a life you love. It is a commitment you must make.

When you make a commitment to yourself, you are establishing a certain standard of achievement for yourself. There are things you will have to accomplish in order for your life to be fulfilled. Since not seeking opportunities and challenges is something you do not want to regret, you will have to be more open to thinking in your best interests and making wise choices.

When it feels like you've gotten off track in life, remember that there is a bigger purpose for your life that only God knows. So although you may wonder why this or that happened, in the scheme of things, it was meant to happen. Everything happens for a reason.

While your life and its fulfillment are the main focus, you also do not want to regret in any way how you did or did not treat others. It is important to treat others as you would want to be treated. When you accomplish things, always give back to others in some way. Live a life in a way that, in the end, you can say, "I loved, I lived, I laughed, I learned, I helped."

LESSON

Live your life in a way that means you never have to look back and wish you could do it differently.

INSPIRATION

—

When you tell me no
I look at you and laugh
you don't know me
like a rubber ball
I bounce higher
when pushed down
I will go farther
than you ever have
reach higher
than you ever dreamed
in spite of
you
in love of
myself
I will achieve
because I must
and for a while
I will throw it in your face
and say ha, ha
you never thought I'd see this place
I'll show you how happiness looks
on a well-deserving face

USE THE DOUBTS OF OTHERS TO PROPEL YOU FORWARD

If someone important to you tends to put you down and doesn't believe in you, it can only help you to achieve great things in life. Take that energy—your anger, your fear, your pain—and use it to make the best of your life. Use it to fuel yourself to want more and show others and yourself that you can accomplish whatever you put your mind to.

Whenever someone attempts to put you down or stifle your life, you can take their ignorance and make it your power. If you want to mentally survive and make something of yourself, you cannot let people have control over your mind or your life. Adopt a kind of "I'll show you" attitude. It's not a way to live your life forever, because eventually you won't care what they think. Until you get to that point, make sure that you turn this type of situation to your advantage and surpass their expectations.

Never hold hate or anger in your heart for anyone. All it does is damage you. It stops you from achieving. It stops you from loving. It stops you from living. Life will correct the pain a person has inflicted on you. It is not up to you to make sure they are hurt the same way they hurt you. You control how you react and how this will affect your life. Above all else, control your life.

LESSON

If anyone attempts to put you down, take it as a challenge to push yourself toward your ultimate dreams.

NO MORE BLUES

———

Like a sickness it is
heart palpitations
racing heart
like a sickness it is
the blues are loved by many
survived by those
who believe themselves to be super
but I'm not super
I'm just me
and this is too much
my heart hurts too much
can't you see
don't you see
the pain in my eyes
can't you describe my life to me
why does this hurt me
who wished this upon me
did I do this to myself
no couldn't be
why is this hurting me

I need to release this
this pain
free me
from myself
before I go
insane

DON'T HOLD ON TO PROBLEMS

We always want to feel like we have control of our lives. We always want to appear as if we have everything together. But no one has his or her life totally together. There are times when you will need others. Even if it is just to talk. Problems are hard to bear when you bear them alone. But once you talk them over with a good friend, you release some of the tension.

Talking to a good friend is therapeutic for you. It is a way to take the anger, pain, or disappointment out of your body. If you hold on to problems and just wonder Why me? it will affect your body and mind. Your body will experience aches and pains. You will begin to believe that only bad things happen to you.

In order to relieve stress, you have to keep it real with yourself and realize that all problems can be overcome or handled in some way. You just have to make sure you have good friends that you can talk with.

The more you focus on a problem, the larger it seems and becomes. When you hold it to yourself and think only you can solve it, you make the process of getting over it take much longer. Even when something seems so painful that you just couldn't tell anyone, you have to trust the love of your friends. Release the pain by sharing it, talking it through, with others. When you talk, you open yourself to receiving love and advice from friends. You learn that you are not the first to deal with a difficult problem. You will see that problems last only as long as it takes to find a solution.

LESSON

You can overcome any problem when you are willing to face it and allow others to help you.

EMBRACE LIFE

A MOMENT OF YOUR TIME

Once you are disbelieved

there is no way of getting back to before

no one wants you

when your time can't be tracked

who cares what happened

this time

it's always the same

you make up things

as if others can't think

so absorbed with yourself

you can't think of anything else

foolish

selfish

girl

no one wants your friendship

no one wants your time

it soured when they were waiting for you

waiting for you to be there

when you said you would

BE RELIABLE

———

You know people who say they're going to be somewhere at a certain time and they show up hours later? Or they never show up at all and give the same tired excuses? You do not want to be one of these people and you want to avoid them at all costs.

No one has respect for people who don't do what they say they're going to do. You cannot excuse this tendency away by saying it's part of someone's personality. It's disrespectful and will not change until you state that it is unacceptable. This person really has no respect for your time or friendship.

When you make a commitment to do something, follow through. If you say you are going to do something or be somewhere, do it. When someone is depending on you, be there for them. Don't try to be everything to everyone, but at least be true to your word.

Being reliable shows people you care about them, their friendship, and that you can be depended on. It shows that you appreciate relationships and can honor commitments. Whether or not you are reliable is a strong indicator of the type of person, worker, and friend you are. If you are not reliable, people will even begin to question the things you say. You will not be believed. Also, when you need someone to be there for you, they may decide not to—just to give you a taste of your own medicine.

LESSON

A reliable person is trustworthy, dependable, and concerned for the well-being of others. Being reliable is being there for someone when they need you.

YOU KNEW BEST

———

Every choice you have made
is right for you
you did what you knew
what you felt
you made the right choice
don't look down
don't give up
the power of God is within you
guiding you
to a life you deserve

NEVER UNDERESTIMATE YOURSELF

As a friend of mine says, every choice was right if you used all the facts and knowledge you had at the time to make the best decision. Accept this idea both because you need to and because it's true. You are not making mistakes—you are living life.

Know that even with your perceived flaws—single parent, not pretty enough, not smart enough, etc.—you are good enough for anyone in this world because God made you. And I'm telling you to believe and know that you are the best and people need to be worthy of you. You are that special. You are that important. You are a gift to them. Remember that.

Don't limit your life. Don't close your life. Don't end your life with thoughts that bring you down emotionally and mentally.

Life can be a wonderful experience if you open yourself up to it. If you are beautiful on the inside, loving, spiritual, caring, and giving, people will want to be around you. It is who we are, who we believe we are, how we are, that brings us what we want, need, and deserve in this life.

There is someone for everyone. There is a wonderful life waiting for you. If you really *want* it, you can have it. Do not think even for a moment that you don't deserve something or someone. You deserve the best.

LESSON

Never stop believing in yourself or the power of God.

QUEEN OF THE WORLD

I believe we are all one

'cept for you

you don't even know where to shop

reject

what are you thinking

that I would even dare speak to you

excuse me

do you think we have something in common

I'm far better

than you

please excuse you

do you know what *condescend* means

I don't have time enough

to do that

so don't even bother speaking to me

I am busy getting in tune

with my spirituality

DON'T PUT OTHERS DOWN

I had a friend who would always put people down. She didn't notice it. And at the time I didn't tell her. She actually thought she was a loving, caring, spiritual person. But she would judge people based on their material possessions or their achievements.

Let me tell you that if you put someone else down, you are putting yourself down. When I tell you to believe in yourself, believe you are the best, I mean that. But that does not mean that you are better than someone else. We all have the spirit of God in us, every last one of us—from a homeless person to a billionaire. We are all the same spirit. We all want love, we all want to be appreciated, and we all want to be needed.

No one is better than anyone else because of any material possession, color, or education. If you are a spiritual person, you do not compare yourself to others or put them down. You do not believe you are better in any way.

Putting others down is literally a disgusting quality. It sounds ugly coming from you. If you were in trouble, you would not want someone to put you down. Instead you would hope someone would have heart enough to acknowledge you and say hi.

Until you feel how wrong it is to treat others badly or to put others down for any reason, until you can look at everyone and say there but for the grace of God go I, you are not living to your full potential nor do you have a true connection with God. God sees the beauty, the spirit, the love in everyone, and, as a part of God, you should be able to do the same. Believe me, it's not difficult. It's just about opening your mind.

Now, when I say love, I do not mean that you have to love everyone. That's not honest. What it means is that everyone deserves and receives God's love; therefore you have no right to put them down. God is within them, just as he is within you.

LESSON

Watch what you proclaim, make sure you are who you say you are.

SHARE YOUR LOVE

IT ALL BEGINS WITH ME

———

Running

running running

around

trying to please my man

my child

my boss

my mother

my father

the stranger on the street

whew I'm tired

ain't got no more to give

oh Jesus

I forgot to give to myself

TRYING TO PLEASE EVERYONE IS A FOOL'S PARADISE

Let's be clear. You cannot, cannot, cannot please everyone. And God knows you shouldn't try. Trying to please everyone is like a dog running in circles trying to catch its tail. It's never going to work.

When you try to please everyone, you're like a puppet on a string. It's like you're running around trying to catch your breath. It's an unhappy, miserable state of being that will stop the minute you say, "Look, you do this yourself." I'm telling you, you're gonna have to go there.

Women especially have a thing about being a super-woman. We can do this, we can do that. Honey, look, what I may be able to do is one thing. What I'm going do is another thing. Life is about me enjoying it, not pleasing others. This may be something that you're going to have to learn.

Your creed should be: "I will do for you what I can, but I will not do more than that." Always give your best, of course. But know when to say when. When you ration your time, you have more energy to do the things you want to do, you give yourself a break in between tasks, and you have time to relax.

I'm known for my long bubble baths. You know why? Because "me time" is important and necessary. Dishes, mail, phone—all that can wait. I sit myself down and recoup. I'm not going to stress for anyone. I'm not going to try to make up for "lost time." I'm not going to try to act like I can do every-thing at any time. Oh no, I know when to say "I'll pass or I'll do it later." Because stress will kill you. You have to know how to relax and when to say no.

There are many ways to be happy. Trying to please others all the time is not one of them. Imagine someone hammering you in the head. That's what you'll feel like if you try to be everything to everyone. Avoid that. Control your life by con-trolling your time and your mind.

LESSON

Overextending yourself can take a toll on your body, your mind, and your spirit. Control your life by being realistic about what you can and cannot do for others. Know when to rejuvenate yourself by relaxing and doing things for you.

STOP AND RUN

Do
what you always do
and you'll get the same s—t
change a thought
you might be surprised
life is what you are willing to make it

In life we can get stuck. We can get set in our ways and lose our focus. But somewhere, somehow, we can still see the hazy, big picture. We can still see that life should be different. We could somehow be different. What you have to do then is stop whatever it is you're doing and run in the right direction.

You have to change the way you think, the way you react, the way you go after things. You don't want to always do the same thing, because then you will always get the same result. So you're going to have to switch cycles to change your life into what you want it to be. To do that sometimes you have to find another way, a better way.

The only way you're going to make a change in your life is when you want it more than anything. You have to break the mold you're stuck in and live life, try life, another way. This isn't to say your life is bad or miserable. It just means that, if it doesn't feel totally right, maybe you should stop and look at your options. Stop and look at what you've been doing and what you could be doing. A rut is the bed of hell. You never want to be caught in one. You never want life to just go the same way every day. Life is a journey, you should enjoy it.

Take a breath. Take a chance and find new things to do with your life. Find ways to challenge and enrich yourself. Find the things you love to do and incorporate them into your life. Don't get stuck doing something you don't even like for the rest of your life. You should love what you do. Hear what I'm saying? You should love what you do. How many people do that? How many people honestly want that?

The difference between honestly wanting and wanting is the desire. If you honestly want it, you're going to find every way to make it happen. If you just want something, you're just dreaming, just wasting time. But wanting something honestly, strongly, is like hunger. You have to fulfill that need. You have to live life to the fullest. That's the only way to enjoy it. That's the only way to love it.

LESSON

You must never lose your desire for life, or the want of a better life. It can be realized if you just change your approach and focus.

MONEY, MONEY, MONEY

Dreams need finance.

From your first week on the job, from the first paycheck, save. Find out about automatic investment plans from mutual fund companies and at least put away fifty dollars a month, minimum. This will pay off for you in the end. You may not think it's much, but it will add up. You have to be prepared for your future. You have to be able to invest in you.

Watch yourself with the credit cards. God knows, there are a lot of sisters with bad credit. My best advice is: Don't use them if you don't have to. Don't be swayed by the free soda on college campuses. Don't be enticed by the low introductory rate. How often would you walk into a bank and ask for a loan with the highest possible interest rate they have? That's what you do every time you use a credit card.

If you have dreams of buying a house, watch yourself with the credit. Don't indulge in shopping to feel better. Don't indulge because you just need that shirt. Keep it real with yourself and use what you have until you can pay cash. Credit really should only be for big-ticket items—a computer or something—but not for your everyday maintenance.

Money is a necessary tool. You need it to get things you want in life. So make sure you save and spend wisely.

LESSON

Money, like emotions, is something you must control to keep your life on the right track.

CIRCLE OF WISDOM

If you know when and where

share that

help a sister out

let me know what you know

so we can keep the legacy

intact

spread the knowledge

like wisdom was carried on our back

take it from railroad philosophy

we all need to get there

some are just more aware

of the stars

spread what you know

help a sister out

SHARE YOUR KNOWLEDGE

—

There's nothing more annoying than a person who has a wealth of knowledge and doesn't share it with her community. If you want the people in the community to be empowered, if you want your community to make better decisions and choices, if you have ideas, knowledge, and wisdom to share, get out there and help. Start a class. Start a workshop. "Each one, teach one" has to be a motto.

People need and want help and sometimes the only way they'll get it is if you jump in. Why acquire knowledge if you're not going to share it? Please, get out there and help somebody learn. Teach somebody what you know. Don't sit up in the house saying the community is going downhill, when you could be helping someone, even one person, get her life on track. It's just not excusable and should be totally unacceptable to you.

It's really horrible how much of our history is stored up in people's brains. Share your experiences. Share them with the community. Children need to know. The community needs to know.

LESSON

Never go so far that you don't know how to go back and give back.

A SPECIAL POEM FOR YOU

I am

my own best friend

my own strength

I am

being pushed

molded

into a beautiful

loving

inspirational

woman

I define my life

God defines my life

I am God's love

manifest

in human form

I will

use the power of God

that resides in me

to create a life

I love

I will give that legacy

of loving myself

to my children

and all that I know

God is within me

I will never forget that

God is within me

I can get through

accomplish

be

anything

that I want to be

I am

my own strength

my own friend

my own love

I am

complete

and powerful

I am beautiful

because my spirit

is based in love

LIFE LESSONS

THE COMPLETE LIST

1. Learn from your experiences.
2. Be open to opportunities.
3. Do not give up on yourself.
4. Go for your highest goal.
5. Believe in yourself.
6. Treat others as you would want to be treated.
7. Your expectations determine your reality.
8. Don't play games with the men you become involved with.
9. Don't expect a man to complete your life.
10. Don't concentrate on marriage, focus instead on having a loving relationship.
11. Don't tell too much about your man.
12. Be aware of your surroundings.

13. Be the chooser, not the chosen.
14. Think about the impact of your decisions before you make them.
15. Notice the subtle clues in your relationships.
16. Don't try to fix anyone.
17. Don't think you can fix or appease the problems your man is having with his family.
18. Love yourself first.
19. Treat your children as precious spirits.
20. Don't fall for love, walk into it with your eyes and heart open.
21. Mama doesn't always know best.
22. Release your negativity and hatred of others.
23. Determine your life—make a life plan.
24. Judge a person on his character and actions, not his words.
25. Don't love for potential, love for right now.
26. Don't get caught up in the moment. Think before you react or act.
27. You can learn from anyone, at any time.
28. Don't envy, emulate.
29. You are what you believe.
30. Make yourself beautiful.
31. Be a role model.
32. You have the power to change the world.
33. What you do will come back to you.
34. Do not lower your standards or your values for anybody.
35. Bitterness will eat away your heart.

36. Be sure you know both sides of a story before you pick a side.
37. Be sure your first is the one you really love.
38. Don't do anything you will regret later.
39. Separate the emotions from the facts to make your decisions.
40. Listen to your heart, think with your brain.
41. Never let anyone abuse you in any way.
42. Your spirit is your motivation.
43. Look at the beauty in life.
44. Cherish your life.
45. At any moment you have the capability of changing your life.
46. Risk is the food of life, it will help you grow.
47. Know what you want out of relationships.
48. Confidence is not an attitude, it's a state of mind.
49. Appreciate where you are.
50. Know who you are.
51. Know your definition of success and happiness.
52. Stick to your values.
53. Do not try to break your man's spirit or change him into what you want him to be.
54. Choose your battles wisely.
55. Expand your horizons—travel, take classes, read.
56. Take care not to become stagnant.
57. Think about the feelings of your friends.
58. Keep some things to yourself.
59. Make life work for you.

60. Know when to listen.
61. Strive to do well at whatever you do or don't do it at all.
62. Appreciate and love yourself.
63. Demand respect through your actions.
64. Exceed the expectations of others.
65. Don't judge yourself or limit yourself by what others believe or perceive of you.
66. You cannot make someone love you, you have to be someone who can be loved.
67. People can influence you only as much as you allow them.
68. Misery loves company.
69. Don't let anyone steal your thunder.
70. Love freely so you can receive free unconditional love.
71. Don't place your hang-ups on somebody else.
72. Don't wait for someone else to make your life better.
73. You are the most important person in the world.
74. God is everywhere, you just have to open your eyes.
75. Before you begin your quest for Mr. Right, make sure you're Ms. Right.
76. Struggle is part of your spiritual evolution.
77. You have to work for what you want.
78. Anyone who can dictate what you do with your life is stifling your spirit and stunting your growth.
79. Give of yourself because it is the spiritual thing to do.
80. Cherish your spirit, feed your spirit.
81. Learn how to forgive.
82. God gives you advice through your intuition.

83. When you listen to your heart (inner voice), you will be happy.

84. Never give up on yourself.

85. Life is meant to be fulfilling.

86. Every decision matters.

87. Become a person you love, then share that love.

88. Know your past.

89. Your career choice is your life choice.

90. Use your fear to your advantage.

91. God is within you, you are within God.

92. Know what you want out of life.

93. Know what you will and will not stand for.

94. Know when to end friendships.

95. Choose a career.

96. Honor your friendships.

97. Look for your inspiration.

98. People are watching your actions.

99. Be real with yourself and with others.

100. Deal with your relationships honestly and openly.

101. Don't be afraid of love.

102. Have sex when you are emotionally and spiritually ready.

103. Save, save, save some money.

104. You define your happiness and your success.

105. Be aware of the lessons in life.

106. Stay focused on your goals.

107. Live on your own, at least once.

108. Do not put others down.

109. Do not let anyone tell you what to do with your life.
110. Be careful of the people who have nothing, because they'll want your something.
111. Take responsibility for your life.
112. Look for opportunities to love.
113. Help others.
114. Recognize your need to change and grow.
115. Recognize your spiritual duty and do it.
116. Seek ways to improve yourself.
117. Break bad habits and addictions.
118. Learn how to live with loss.
119. Decide to find happiness within yourself.
120. Share your knowledge.
121. Love what you do.
122. Be aware of people's motivations.
123. Know when to move on.
124. Life is a journey, enjoy every moment.
125. Create success for yourself.

MY LIFE

I'VE BEEN THROUGH SO MANY THINGS that I've become my own best friend, my own strength. I tell myself what I need to hear. I inspire myself. I remind myself of how special I am.

I know that with all the lessons God has given me, there is an ultimate reason. There will be a day when I can say that's why that happened. I know he's not giving up on me. Just pushing me, molding me, to become the person I need to be.

God is the only one I will allow to define my life. God's presence is strongly within me, inside my heart. I try to give that pure love to others. I try to show people how much I love and care about them. I want people in my life to know they are loved. And I'll be there for them when they need me. I love them completely.

My strength to get through life is fueled by my desire and my love. I want a better life, therefore I can't allow anyone to hurt the process. I need to be happy. I need to be me. So I can never stop and let life get to me. I can't sit for long and say, "Why me?" I can never tell myself there's no way of getting out of this.

I will always find a way to achieve, to love, to be me. I have to! It is as essential to me as my breath. God gave me so much that I have to give something back.

I have to show God that I appreciate the life he gave me. And I will become that person I am destined to be. I will fulfill every dream, one step at a time. I will never close my mind to life or love.

I will feel the moment. I will feel the pain, the joy, the heartache, the love, the crying, and the laughing. I will feel life. Live it to its fullest. So I can be fulfilled, and give my love. There's no other way for me to be.

My dreams are the precious essence of my mind. My talent is my strength. The love I can give is beautiful because I love myself so much.

No one can hurt me more than I can hurt myself. No one will ever abuse or use me. It's unacceptable. My life will not be defined by that.

Even at my weakest moment I am my best strength. I have the power to shape my life. I have the love to heal my heart. I have the ability to change everything.

God is within me and I will never forget that. God is within me and I can get through anything, accomplish anything, be anything that I want to be.

I am my own strength. My own friend. My own love. So I never lose because I have me.

We are all complete in that way. We just have to feel it. Remember it. Honor it. We have everything we need inside of us.

We are the love of God manifest in human form. We are so powerful. We just need to know it.

Everything you need is inside of you. Bring it out. Bring out the God. Bring out the love. Acknowledge your spirit.

Always remember, spirituality is not saying you're better than others, it is not turning your back on your fellow man. It is not about putting others down or judging or limiting them to your expectations.

Spirituality is opening your heart to love and allowing yourself to learn from every individual. It is knowing that God wants the best for you, that God is within you—and everybody else—and therefore you can make the world a better place by simply being you and allowing God to flow through you and touch the lives of others.

I wish you the very best on your search for the most powerful love—the love that is inside of you. I hope you find it one day and realize how magnificent you are.

Live a life you love!

Natasha Munson

I would love to hear from you. E-mail Natasha@sister lessons.com or check out www.sisterlessons.com for contact and other project information.

ABOUT THE AUTHOR

Natasha Munson is a motivational speaker with a focus on empowering the community one spirit at a time. She resides in Atlanta, Georgia, with her two daughters.

Take action to change your financial, spiritual, and emotional life forever!

Lesson #6
If you want love, you must give love.

Lesson #28
Commit to your happiness.

Lesson #62
You always have the ability to change your life.

Lesson #75
Things will always work out.

"Natasha Munson has all the answers."
–*Black Beat*

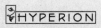